The Jodie Davis Needle Arts School

◆ **THE FOUNDATION PIECING LIBRARY** ◆

HEARTS AND FLOWERS

◆

QUILT BLOCK DESIGNS

The Jodie Davis Needle Arts School

◆ **THE FOUNDATION PIECING LIBRARY** ◆

HEARTS AND FLOWERS

◆

QUILT BLOCK DESIGNS

JODIE DAVIS AND LINDA HAMPTON SCHIFFER

FRIEDMAN/FAIRFAX
PUBLISHERS

A FRIEDMAN/FAIRFAX BOOK

Library of Congress Cataloging-in-Publication Data

Davis, Jodie, date
    Hearts and flowers quilt block designs / Jodie Davis and Linda Hampton Schiffer.
        p.   cm. – (Jodie Davis needle arts school) (The foundation piecing library)
    Includes bibliographical references and index.
    ISBN 1-56799-443-1
        1. Patchwork–Patterns.   2. Patchwork quilts.   3. Love in art.
    4. Heart in art.   I. Schiffer, Linda Hampton.   II. Title.
    III. Series.   IV. Series: Davis, Jodie, 1959-   Jodie Davis needle arts school.
    TT835. D3746   1997
    746.46'041–DC20   96-38477

Editor: Francine Hornberger
Art Director: Lynne Yeamans
Designer: Tanya Ross-Hughes
Photography Director: Christopher C. Bain
Production Manager: Camille Lee

Photography by Christopher C. Bain
Illustrations by Barbara Hennig

Color separations by HBM Print Ltd.
Printed in China by Leefung-Asco Printers Ltd.

Every effort has been made to present the information in this book in a clear, complete, and accurate manner. It is important that all
instructions be clearly understood before beginning a project. Please follow instructions carefully. Due to the variability of materials and
skills, end results may vary. The publisher and the authors expressly disclaim any and all liability resulting from injuries, damages, or
other losses incurred as a result of material presented herein. The authors also suggest refraining from using glass, beads, or buttons on
quilt blocks or projects created for small children.

1 3 5 7 9 10 8 6 4 2

For bulk purchases and special sales, please contact:
Friedman/Fairfax Publishers
Attention: Sales Department
15 West 26th Street
New York, New York 10010
212/685-6610   FAX 212/685-1307

Visit our website:
http://www.metrobooks.com

To Skip, who is always there for me.

—Linda Hampton Schiffer

ACKNOWLEDGMENTS

Thanks to Pat Steiner of the wonderful quilt shop Cottonseed Glory in Annapolis, Maryland, where the fabric for this book was purchased.

To Jeanne Welch, our applause for so skillfully stitching Linda's designs into blocks, and to Kathy Semone who labored so willingly to make the sample quilts.

CONTENTS

INTRODUCTION

WHAT IS FOUNDATION PIECING?

Foundation piecing is simply the fastest and by far the easiest method ever devised for constructing quilt blocks—so easy, in fact that even a complete beginner can make beautiful blocks. It's foolproof!

THE PROCESS IN A NUTSHELL

The blocks are constructed by machine sewing along lines drawn on a paper or fabric foundation. The foundation provides stability, the lines accuracy.

First, the block design is transferred to the foundation. With the marked lines face up, two pieces of fabric, right sides together, are placed under the foundation and stitched to the foundation

along the marked line. The two fabric pieces are pressed open, into place. More pieces are added until the block is complete. Finally, the blocks are sewn together, and voilá—a completed quilt top.

THE PATTERNS

The patterns included in this, the third in The Foundation Piecing Library series, are based on images that invoke romance. Hearts, flowers, cuddly animals, butterflies, and more combine in a potpourri of romantic block designs.

All of the block designs and quilting projects are rated for ease of construction, designated by the number of diamonds appearing on the page they first appear. If you are just beginning, select a pattern from those featuring one diamond. The most challenging patterns have three. The photographs of the blocks include their ¼" (6mm) seam allowances.

Foundation pieced blocks are the perfect opportunity for you to use those precious scraps of fabric you've been saving. And remember not to limit yourself to the block size offered in the book. Page 15 provides a chart to help you easily enlarge or reduce a block pattern.

THE QUILTS AND PROJECTS

The five quilt designs and valentine project, each using one or more of the patterns from the Block Patterns section, are offered in the Quilt and Accessory Designs section. These will provide the perfect opportunity to put your new skills to use in creating a finished project.

What could be easier? No templates, no marking, no painstaking cutting. Foundation piecing is easy enough for a beginner, yet challenges the seasoned quilter. Above all, foundation piecing offers accuracy and speed. And it's fun!

JODIE DAVIS

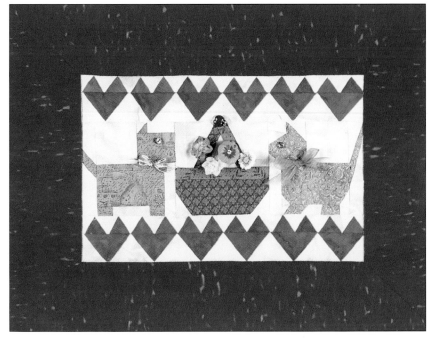

CHAPTER ONE

FOUNDATION PIECING PRIMER

This chapter provides all the information you need to make the quilt blocks in this book. The only requirement is that you can sew along a straight, drawn line with your sewing machine. That's it!

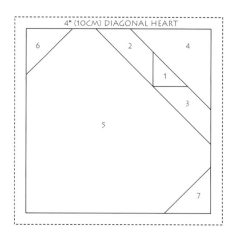

CALLING ALL HAND PIECERS

These patterns make excellent carry-along projects for trips, in waiting rooms, and after-school practice waits. Only a few sewing supplies and small scraps are needed.

For hand piecing, a fabric foundation is strongly recommended. Paper is too difficult to sew through by hand.

NOTE: You will be sewing from the wrong side of the blocks. The marked side of the foundation is the wrong side. For this reason the finished block will be a mirror image of the drawn designs in this book. Notice that for asymmetrical blocks, the photos of the blocks are in fact mirror images of the drawn block. For symmetrical blocks, there will be no difference between the drawn and sewn blocks.

THE DESIGNS

The block and border designs in this book are full-size, and all are ready to be traced and used. The numbers on the blocks indicate the sewing sequence for the fabric pieces.

The lines on the block designs represent the sewing lines. A dashed ¼" (6mm) seam allowance has been added all around the outside of each block.

Asymmetrical block

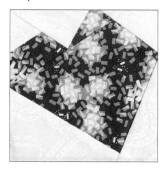

Symmetrical block

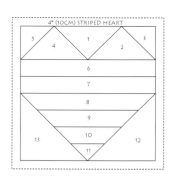

FOUNDATION OPTIONS

Foundations can be either permanent or temporary, depending upon the desired end result or working method (hand versus machine).

PERMANENT FOUNDATIONS

A fabric foundation is permanent. The patchwork pieces are stitched to the base fabric, which is usually muslin. The foundation then becomes an additional layer in the quilt sandwich. A benefit for some projects (for instance, to add body to a wall hanging or vest), a fabric foundation isn't the best choice for others, such as a project calling for extensive hand quilting or a miniature that shouldn't be too stiff.

Choose good-quality muslin for your foundations, and be sure to prewash, especially if the finished project will be laundered.

CREATIVE OPTIONS: For exciting and unusual quilts, play with block orientation and combinations. Look at the patterns, their mirror (flipped) images, and combinations of both. Plan for the final block/quilt design that you want. To do this easily, use a photocopy machine to make several copies of the selected block pattern, then arrange and rearrange these blocks until you like the result.

NOTE: When using a fabric foundation, cut the foundation square with the grainline of the fabric.

TEMPORARY FOUNDATIONS

Paper of many types is an excellent, inexpensive foundation. It provides more stability for piecing than muslin and eliminates the additional layer of a permanent fabric foundation, allowing for easier hand quilting. After construction, the paper is removed from the completed block by tearing. In some cases, this can cause fraying of seam allowances and distortion of the block; also, some bits of paper may remain stuck in the stitches. You can avoid these problems by using a shorter stitch length. This way, removing the paper will be similar to tearing postage stamps apart.

Leave the paper foundation in place until after you piece the blocks together. Blocks will be easier to align, and won't become distorted by tearing the paper away. This also eliminates concern about the grainline of the block edges.

Almost any paper is appropriate for foundation piecing. Copy, computer, and typing paper are readily obtainable. Available in grocery stores, freezer paper is favored by many quilters. The dull side of the paper is marked with the block pattern and the shiny side is pressed to fabric with a dry iron and a press cloth. Tracing paper has the advantage of lighter weight, so stitches won't distort as readily when the paper is torn away.

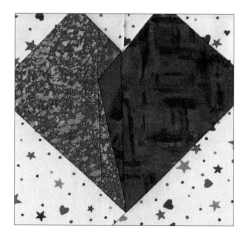

TRANSFERRING THE BLOCK DESIGNS

To reproduce the block designs on paper, trace or photocopy the desired pattern from this book. When tracing, use a ruler to ensure accuracy. Be sure to copy the piecing sequence numbers as well.

A copy machine makes quick work of reproducing patterns. To test the precision of the copies, make one copy of a block and measure to be sure the size is correct. Cut along the outside, dashed lines.

NOTE: If you use a photocopier to enlarge a block to another size, you'll need to redraw the seam allowance so that it's ¼" (6mm).

To transfer block designs to fabric, you may place the muslin over the block design on a light table or tape the design to a sunny window. Trace using permanent fabric tools. As an alternative, use heat transfer pens and pencils to speed the marking of fabric foundations. Following the manufacturer's instructions, make a transfer on paper and check it for accuracy. You can then make multiple replicas on fabric or paper using the same transfer.

NOTE: Be sure to use marking tools such as a pencil or permanent fabric pens when marking the fabric foundations. Pigma and Pilot SC-UF are good examples of the latter (see Sources). If the ink used is not stable it can bleed into the block front during construction or after the quilt is complete.

BLOCKS IN ANY SIZE

If you require block sizes other than those offered, start with the 4" (10cm) block and refer to the following chart to adjust the size; remember to adjust the seam allowances to ¼" (6mm) all around.

For a block size of:	Set the copy machine to:
2" (5cm)	50%
3" (7.5cm)	75%
5" (12.5cm)	125%
6" (15cm)	150%
8" (20cm)	200%

FABRICS

Fabric shops offer a delicious variety of fabrics for the quilter. High-quality all-cotton fabrics used in traditional quilting are a joy to work with and have a timeless appeal.

Many quilters are exploring the possibilities of such nontraditional fabrics as lamé, flannel, and unusual blends. For flimsy fabrics such as tissue lamé, fuse interfacing to the back of the fabric before use (tricot-backed lamés are preferred as they don't fray, nor do they require backing with interfacing). A muslin foundation will give thin, delicate fabrics the extra support they require.

PREPARING FABRICS

If you are using small scraps to make blocks, be sure each piece is at least ¾" (2cm) larger than the final patch dimensions. If in doubt, put the fabric against the back of the printed pattern and hold it up to the light.

For larger scraps or new yardage, cut strips at least ¾" (2cm) wider than the desired final patch. Or, cut strips 6" (15cm) wide for 4" (10cm) blocks; these can be cut into strips across the length to fit specific patch spaces as needed.

SEWING

For paper piecing set your sewing machine to 18 to 20 stitches per inch (2.5cm) or a stitch setting of 1½, depending upon the make of your machine. The short stitch length creates closely spaced perforations that will facilitate tearing away the paper, if that is your choice of foundation. Simultaneously, it stabilizes the seam.

Use an 80/12 needle. If you use a paper foundation, switch to a 90/14 needle if you have trouble tearing the paper away.

Choose your thread according to the fabrics selected. Light gray is a good choice for assorted lighter fabrics; dark gray for black prints and darker fabrics.

If you have trouble mentally flipping the image at first, carefully baste along each line on your chosen foundation *with no thread* in your machine using your longest stitch length. Now you will be able to see exactly where the seam will be, even when viewing the unprinted block face.

For final machine assembly of the quilt top use your normal stitch length.

When making multiple blocks of a pattern, Karen Kraft of Caledonia, MI constructs the blocks assembly-line fashion. She sews piece #1 for each block first, then piece #2 for every block, etc.

FOUNDATION PIECING METHOD

To demonstrate the foundation piecing method, I have chosen one of the easiest blocks in the book as an example. Follow these steps to make your own practice block.

REMEMBER: The marked side of the paper will be at the back of the finished block. Therefore, the finished block will be a mirror image of the drawn pattern.

For smoother seams and fabric that's easier to handle, use spray sizing on your completed blocks before assembling them.
—Ellen Robinson, Germantown, MD

If you have trouble seeing the drawn line when sewing, switch to a clear or open toe foot on your sewing machine.

2. Cut a piece of fabric for piece #2. Pin piece #2 against piece #1, right sides facing and adjacent edges even. Working from the marked back, stitch along the marked line; begin and end the stitching a few stitches beyond the ends of the line.

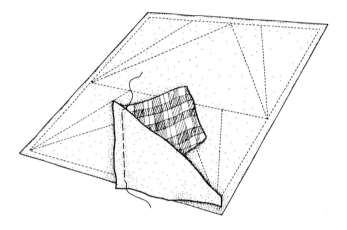

1. Starting with the shape marked #1 on the pattern, place the fabric you've chosen for piece #1 with the wrong side against the unmarked side of the foundation paper or fabric. Hold the foundation and fabric up to a light source to help you see the marked lines. Pin in place. Make sure the fabric covers the shape with at least ¼" (6mm) extending over the marked line all around. Be generous with the fabric: it's better to have too big a piece now than to come up short later.

3. Trim the seam allowances to ¼" (6mm). For blocks 2" (5cm) square or smaller, trim to ⅛" (3mm).

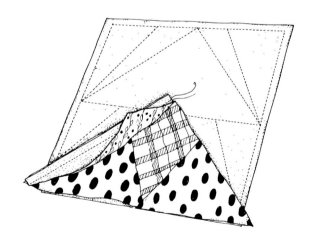

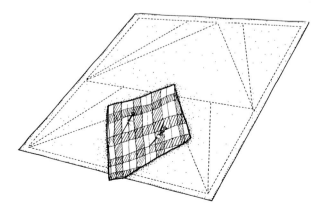

NOTE: Be careful not to cut the foundation when trimming seam allowances. Feel for the foundation with your fingers or scissors—or look. It will save you a lot of grief!

4. Fold piece #2 into place and finger press. Then press with a dry iron—no steam. In the same manner, add the third and all subsequent pieces, pressing as you go.

Instead of pinning the subunits together at the match points, try using vinyl-coated paper clips to hold the blocks together.

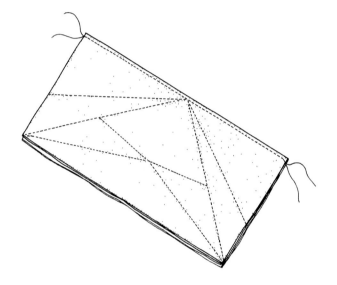

5. Using a rotary cutter and a ruler or square template, trim the edges of the block along the dashed lines. This leaves a ¼" (6mm) seam allowance all the way around the block.

OPTIONAL: Some quilters baste around the finished block from the right side, just inside the seam allowances. This anchors the fabric pieces so that they won't move out of place when you're joining the blocks.

SUBUNIT BLOCKS

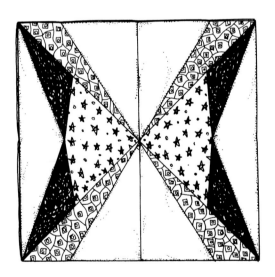

A few block designs consist of two (or more) pieces, such as two triangles or rectangles (subunits). The two subunits are prepared using foundation piecing techniques and then joined together to make a complete 4" (10cm) block, matching points and seams where necessary.

WHAT ABOUT THE GRAINLINE?

For all patchwork it is important to be aware of fabric grain considerations. Fabric is woven and you can easily see the intersecting threads, or grainlines. The lengthwise grain (parallel to the selvedges) has less "give" or elasticity than the crosswise (perpendicular to the selvedges) grain. If you pull a piece of fabric diagonally (at a 45-degree angle) to the grain, you will get a lot of stretching—this is the bias. When you assemble patchwork blocks, you should be aware that placing bias edges at the outside edges of the block will allow a block to stretch easily. The resulting variance of edge lengths will hinder easy joining of the blocks and prevent your quilt from hanging or laying straight.

One of the real virtues of foundation piecing is that this concern with grainline can be minimized. When using a permanent fabric foundation, be sure your pattern is applied to the foundation fabric even with the thread lines. Then you will not need to be concerned at all with the grainline of any of the patchwork fabrics you use to make your block. In addition, you can orient the printed pattern on your patch fabric to please your eye, with no concern for grain.

However, if you use a paper foundation and wish to remove the paper before final quilt assembly, you need to be careful not to put bias edges along the outer seam lines of your blocks. You can leave the paper foundations on the blocks until after assembly to alleviate this worry over outer bias edges. Be aware that paper removal can be tedious when working with a completed top. You may find a good pair of tweezers helpful in the paper removal task.

STITCH AND TUCK TRICK

Seven of the blocks (Playful Kitty, Ice Cream Sundae, Picnic Basket, Head Over Heels, Butterfly III, Love Bird, and Falling in Love) make use of a simple folding technique which allows you to negotiate a point without piecing.

Simply sew the seam as if it were straight, stop at the point with your needle down in the fabric and pivot, then continue on. Trim the seam allowances normally, then turn the fabric to the right side. Because you stitched the point, there will be a bit of extra fabric which you will then press into a pleat. If you wish, you may ladderstitch the fold of the pleat, though this is optional.

♦ CHAPTER TWO ♦

BLOCK PATTERNS

BLOCK PATTERNS

Saint Valentine, the patron saint of lovers, was martyred on February 14 in the year 270 A.D. for defying the orders of the Roman emperor Claudius II, who had decided to ban all engagements and marriages between Roman citizens. The emperor thought that forbidding romantic involvements would make his soldiers more willing to go off to war. Valentine, an early Christian priest, continued to secretly marry those who sought him. About two hundred years after his death, Saint Valentine's Day became a feast day for celebrating married love. Today, lovers still celebrate Valentine's Day to commemorate the power of romance.

In this, our third book in the Foundation Piecing Library series, we have chosen to focus on block patterns with a hearts and flowers theme. But these designs encompass more than affairs of the heart: friendship and family ties are also celebrated.

As we are living busier and more complex lives, with greater obstacles to overcome to maintain our human connections and nurture our relationships, we have come to express our love and concern for others in different ways than was necessary when our circle of contacts might have been confined to our local community. We can easily show those we love how much we care by making tokens of friendship and good will for our siblings, children, parents, or other friends to celebrate birthdays, anniversaries, or other significant events.

The most obvious romantic quilt we may construct is one that celebrates or expresses the bond between lovers. Successful, long-lasting romantic relationships require not just an active courtship period but also maintenance of the heart. Whether you are making a love token to celebrate a new love or a deep and abiding relationship, I hope you can find a pattern that satisfies your intent in this volume.

It is not always necessary to make full-size quilts with these blocks. You can make small items like sachets and pillows in thanks for favors done or as hostess gifts. Smaller quilts could be used as invitations to a special event or as mementos of some shared pleasure. A special tea party or picnic for a few choice friends could be announced with small fabric items. We can celebrate the strength of shared teamwork with a fabric memory to the other participants. A small but lasting thank-you for a friendly gesture, recognition for a job well done—there are many opportunities in life for recognizing and expressing our positive feelings. Indeed, in so acknowledging our feelings to others, we maintain the essence of our human connectedness.

While you are planning your fabric statement, please remember to enjoy the process of production as well as the final product. Take pleasure in your choice of fabrics. Play with cool versus warm colors. Experiment with fabric types. Don't overlook the use of stripes, plaids, florals of many scales, geo-metrics, or hand-produced fabrics. Focus on whether you want a serene or energetic final quilt and choose your colors and textures accordingly. Think, too, of the iconic tokens of romance and friendship—flowers, hearts, hands, tea parties, picnics. I hope you will find designs that will allow you to express your feelings in fabric to those you care about.

To the right is a script alphabet sized for the areas intended for lettering in several of the friend-ship quilt blocks. Trace these letters onto a light-colored fabric or muslin and pen the letters in with permanent marker—I suggest a Pigma pen (see Sources)—before constructing your quilt block.

LINDA HAMPTON SCHIFFER

SCRIPT ALPHABET

A B C D
E F G H I
J K L M N
O P Q R S
T U V
W X Y Z
a b c d e f g
h i j k l m n
o p q r s t u
v w x y z

BLOCK DESIGN COMMENTS

♦ = easy
♦♦ = modest difficulty
♦♦♦ = challenging

STANDING HEARTS

Nothing symbolizes romance better than a heart. Use these blocks to make a special Valentine quilt.

STRIPED HEART ♦

A gradation of colors will make a beautiful rainbow for this heart.

LARGE UPRIGHT HEART ♦

Use brilliant fabrics with this simple heart pattern to make a memorable statement.

BRAIDED HEART ♦

Choose your fabrics thoughtfully to give this block that wrapped-in-love look.

CRAZY HEART ◆

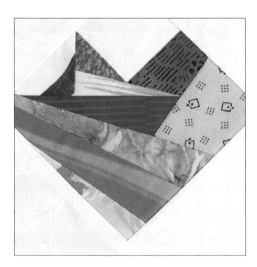

BEATING HEART ◆

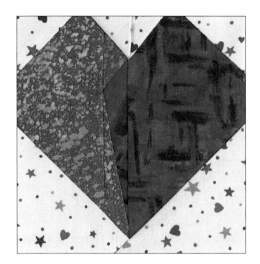

For an old-time crazy quilt look, make this block on a fabric foundation using an assortment of silks, velvets, or lace. Embroider over seam lines for an authentic touch.

Two contrasting fabrics will make this heart appear to beat wildly.

PUZZLE HEART I ◆

FLOWER OF LOVE HEART ◆

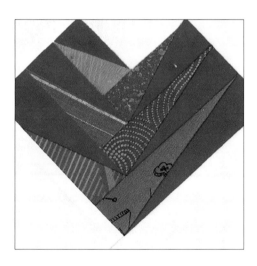

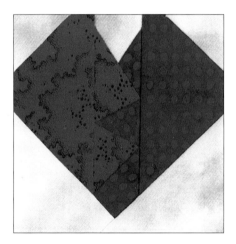

Remember those separating charms you used to share with your most special friends? Put yours back together in this block.

Some days we are all prickles and thorns, even to the ones we love. This heart block will make for a great apology.

DOUBLE HEART ♦ ♦

Keep your loved one safe in your heart. Choose fabrics with colors or prints that hold special meaning to each of you and that have good contrast.

HEART AND HOME ♦ ♦

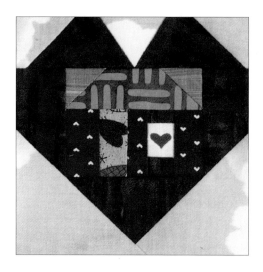

Love of hearth and home is basic to security and happiness. Express your feelings with this pattern.

HEART FRAME BLOCK ♦ ♦

When you use solid fabric for the internal square, this block is a good one for calligraphy and poetry.

PATRIOT AT HEART ♦ ♦

Your strong patriotic feelings will shine through with this easy pattern.

HEAD OVER HEELS ♦ ♦ ♦

Falling in love is a dizzying experience, but exciting all the same. Use joyful colors in this pattern for a glorious result.

KEY TO MY HEART ♦ ♦

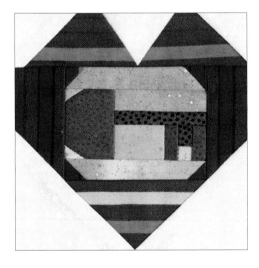

Give the key to your heart to your valentine this year with this special block.

LARGE UPRIGHT HEART

Creative options

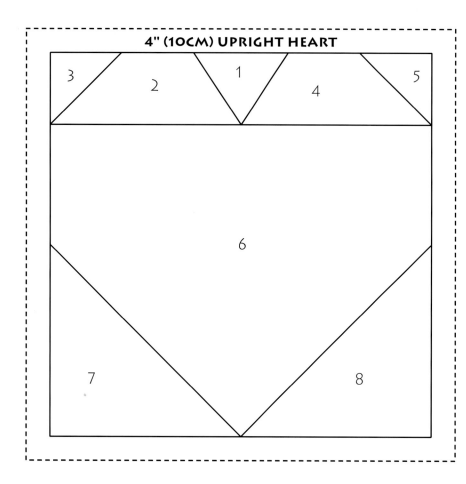

4" (10CM) UPRIGHT HEART

3 2 1 4 5

6

7 8

STRIPED HEART

Creative options

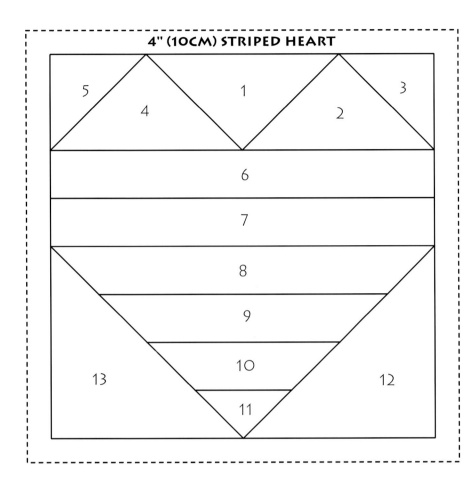

4" (10CM) STRIPED HEART

5   1   3
4   2
6
7
8
9
10
13   12
11

BRAIDED HEART

Creative options

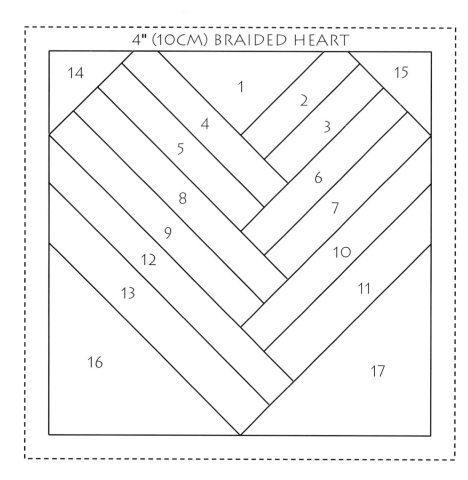

4" (10CM) BRAIDED HEART

14   1   15

2

4   3

5

6

8   7

9

10

12

13   11

16   17

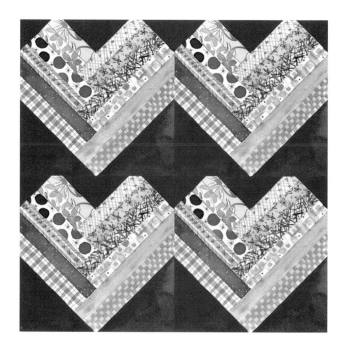

CRAZY HEART

Creative options

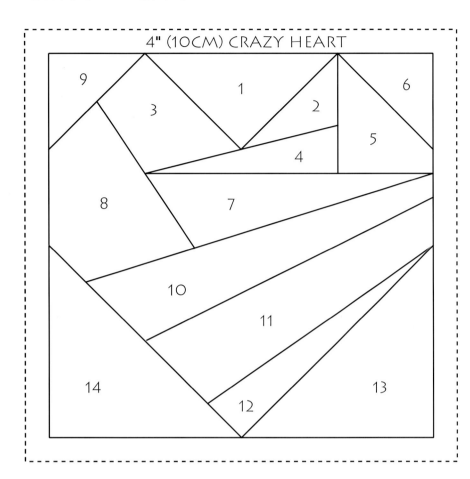

4" (10CM) CRAZY HEART

9   1   6
3   2
  4   5
8   7
10
11
14   13
12

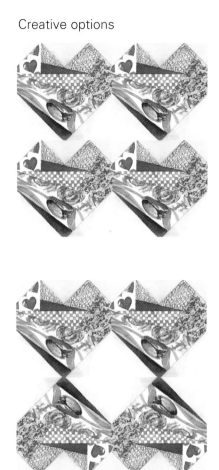

FLOWER OF LOVE HEART

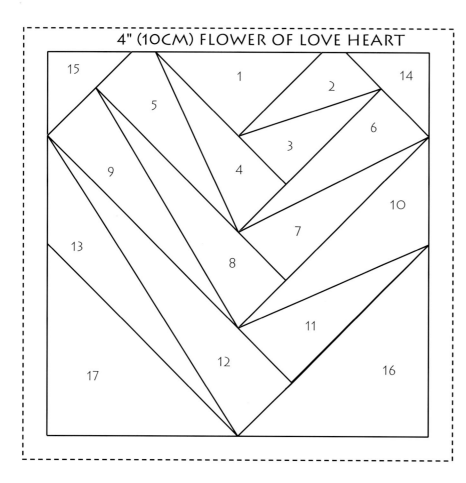

4" (10CM) FLOWER OF LOVE HEART

15 1 2 14
5
3
4 6
9
7
10
13
8
11
17 12 16

Creative options

BEATING HEART

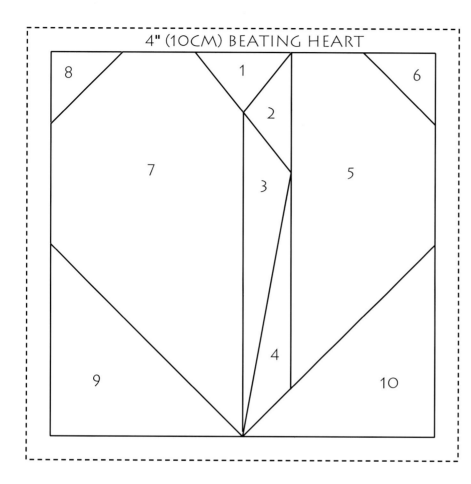

4" (10CM) BEATING HEART

8 | 1 | 6
7 | 2 | 5
  | 3 |
  | 4 |
9 | | 10

Creative options

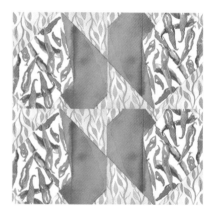

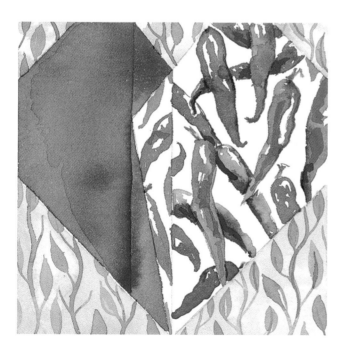

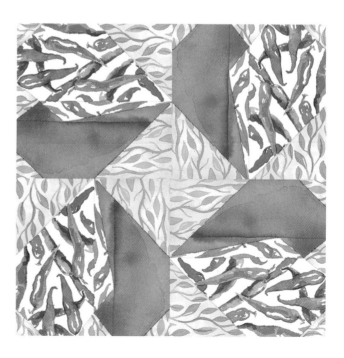

PUZZLE HEART I

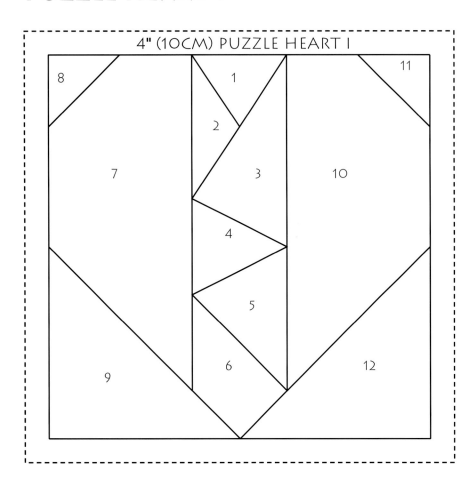

4" (10CM) PUZZLE HEART I

8
1
2
7
3
10
4
5
9
6
12
11

Creative options

DOUBLE HEART

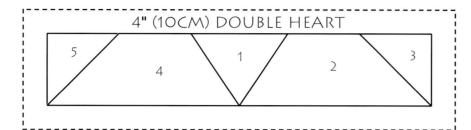

4" (10CM) DOUBLE HEART

Creative options

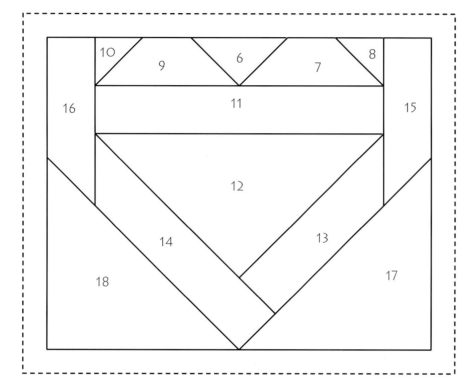

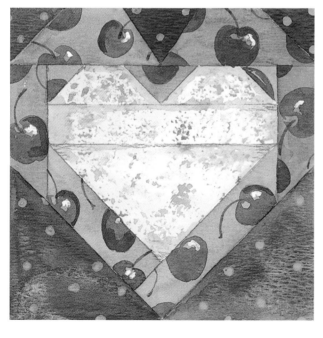

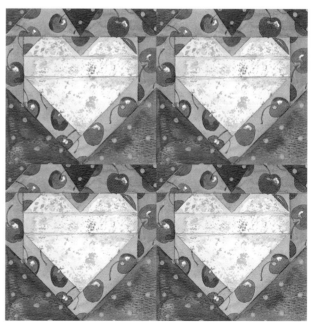

HEART FRAME BLOCK

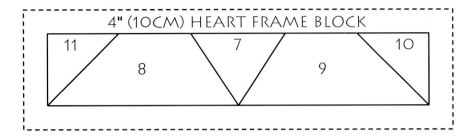

4" (10CM) HEART FRAME BLOCK

11   7   10
8
9

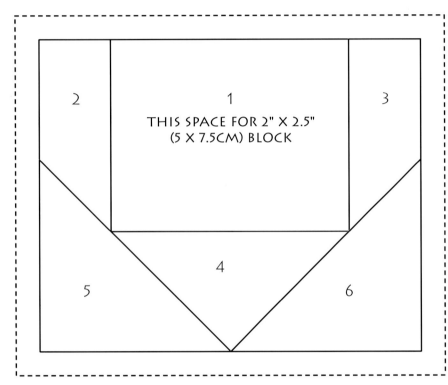

2   1   3

THIS SPACE FOR 2" X 2.5"
(5 X 7.5CM) BLOCK

4

5   6

THIS BLOCK CAN BE
USED TO FEATURE
A SPECIAL FABRIC MOTIF,
LACE, EMBROIDERY,
LETTER MESSAGE,
OR PHOTO TRANSFER.
YOU CAN USE THE
INSERTION PATTERNS
ON PAGES 38–39, OR THE
SCRIPT ALPHABET ON
PAGE 23 TO SEND
A SPECIAL MESSAGE.

Creative options

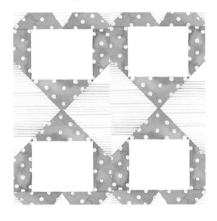

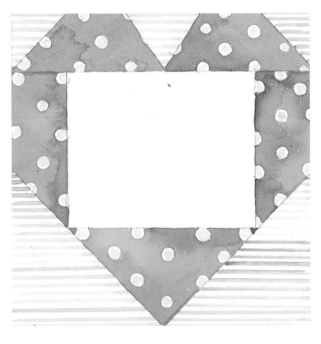

HEART AND HOME
(INSERTION PATTERN)

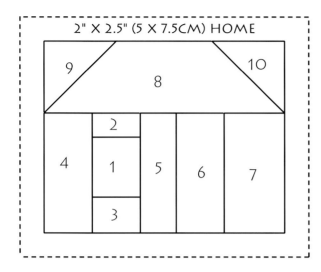

2" X 2.5" (5 X 7.5CM) HOME

Suggested use in Heart Frame (page 36)

PATRIOT AT HEART
(INSERTION PATTERN)

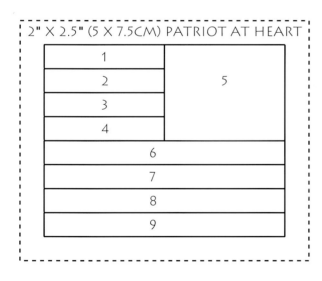

2" X 2.5" (5 X 7.5CM) PATRIOT AT HEART

Suggested use in Heart Frame (page 36)

KEY TO MY HEART

(INSERTION PATTERN)

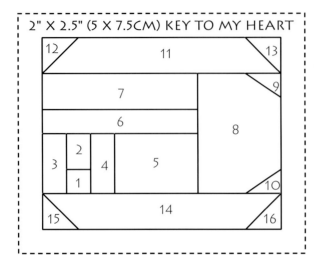

2" X 2.5" (5 X 7.5CM) KEY TO MY HEART

Suggested use in Heart Frame (page 36)

Creative options

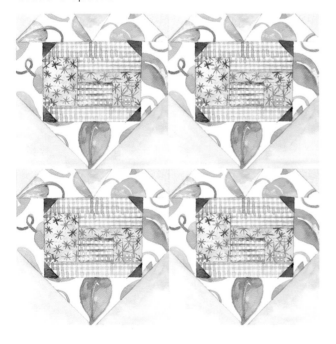

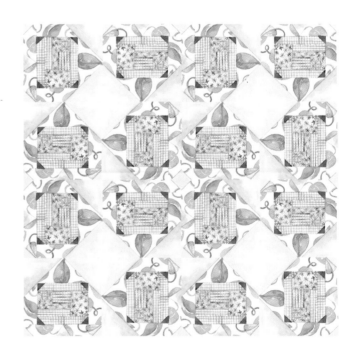

HEAD OVER HEELS

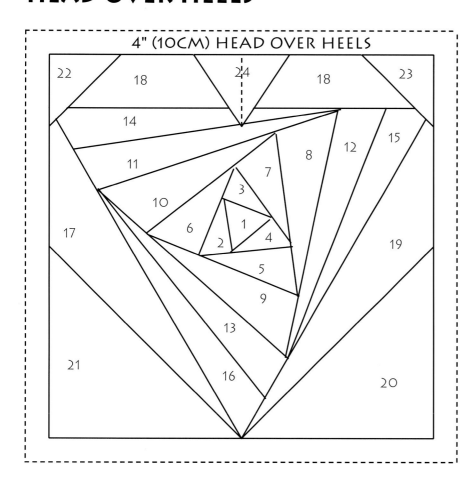

4" (10CM) HEAD OVER HEELS

SEW PIECE 18 AS ONE STRIP. SEW PIECE 24 ON TOP OF PIECES 14 AND 18. AFTER SEWING PIECE 24, DOTTED LINE SHOWS PLACEMENT OF FOLD WHEN PRESSING PIECE UPWARD; TRIM EXCESS FABRIC.

NOTE: TO SEW PIECE 24, SEE PAGE 19 FOR "STITCH AND TUCK TRICK."

Creative option

HEARTS ON POINT

These slanted hearts will create visual interest and fun in your next quilt.

HEARTTHROB ◆

Use dazzling colors to make a quilt bursting with energy and excitement for your heartthrob.

DIAGONAL HEART ◆

This simple pattern is smashing when made in a wide range of colors and patterns: try Amish brights, country florals, hand-dyed solids, or wild contemporary prints.

DIAGONAL HEART FRAME ◆

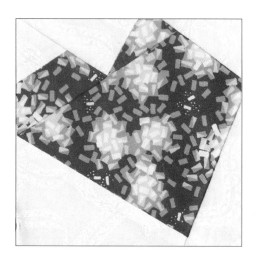

You can spell out your special Valentine message in this special heart frame using the script alphabet on page 23.

DIAGONAL STRIPED HEART ◆ ◆

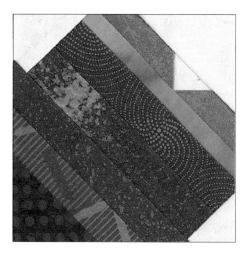

Irregular strips allow for a number of different fabric tricks. Consider sewing charms or tiny prairie points onto this block.

DIAGONAL BRAIDED
HEART ◆ ◆

Try shading fabrics from dark to light in either direction for a memorable result in this pattern.

DIAGONAL DOUBLE
HEART ◆ ◆

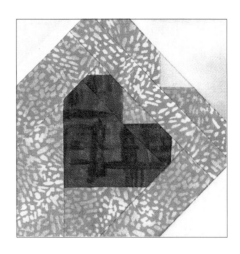

Fabrics with good contrast will give the best results when making this block for someone you hold dear.

DIAGONAL CRAZY
HEART ◆ ◆

The patch shapes in this pattern may be embellished with silk ribbon or floss embroidery, painting, or calligraphy. Let your imagination run wild and create a truly striking crazy quilt.

PUZZLE HEART II ♦ ♦

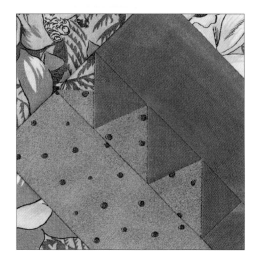

Like medieval betrothal rings that were sometimes made as interlocking puzzle pairs, this pattern will relay a message of togetherness with love.

STRING OF HEARTS ♦ ♦ ♦

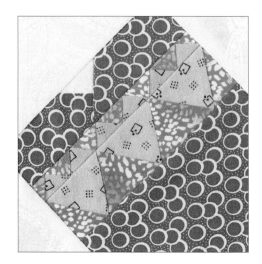

Show someone just how much you love him or her with this pattern created from multiple hearts.

HEARTTHROB

4" (10cm) HEARTTHROB

2
3
4
6
1
5
7
8

Creative options

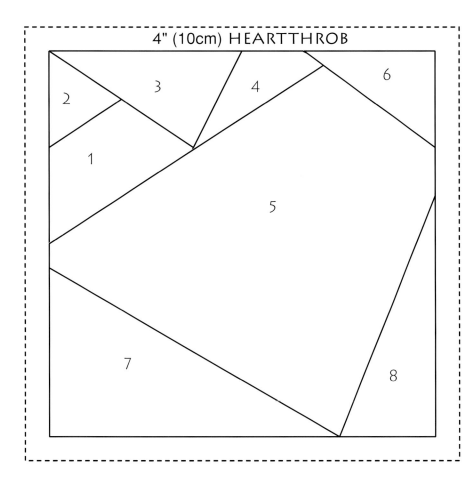

DIAGONAL HEART

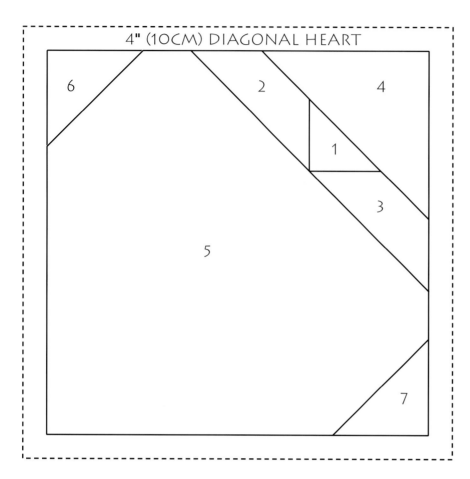

4" (10CM) DIAGONAL HEART

6 2 4

1

3

5

7

Creative options

2" (5CM) DIAGONAL HEART

6 2 4

1

3

5

7

DIAGONAL HEART FRAME

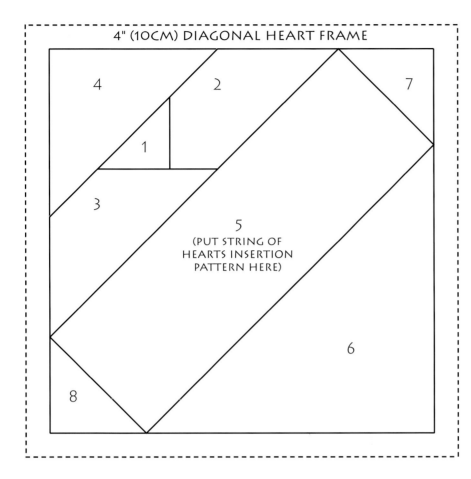

4" (10CM) DIAGONAL HEART FRAME

4

2

7

1

3

5

(PUT STRING OF
HEARTS INSERTION
PATTERN HERE)

6

8

Creative options

DIAGONAL STRIPED HEART

4" (10CM) DIAGONAL STRIPED HEART

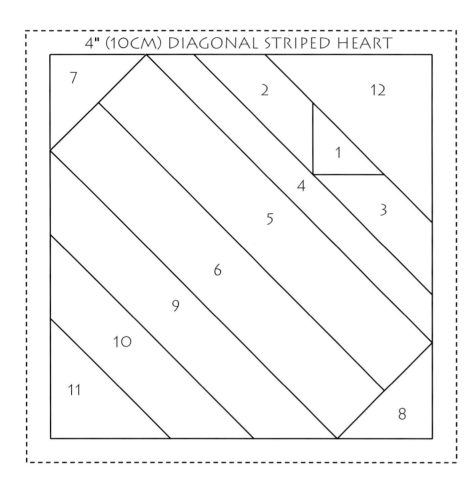

Creative options

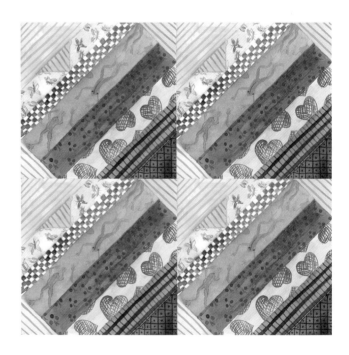

DIAGONAL BRAIDED HEART

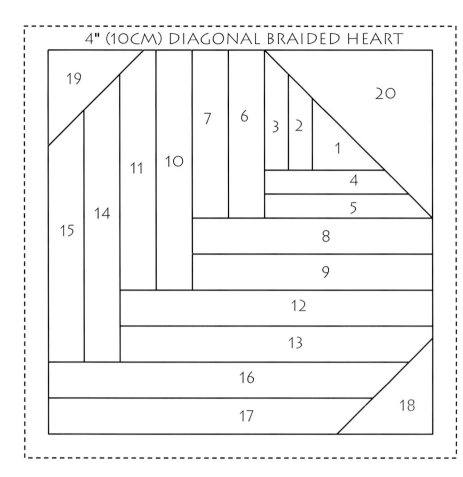

4" (10CM) DIAGONAL BRAIDED HEART

Creative options

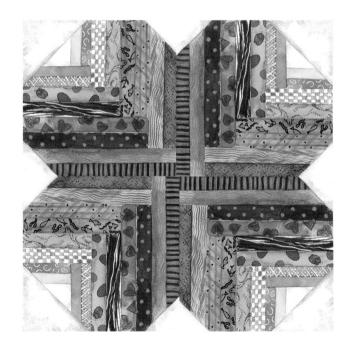

DIAGONAL CRAZY HEART

Creative options

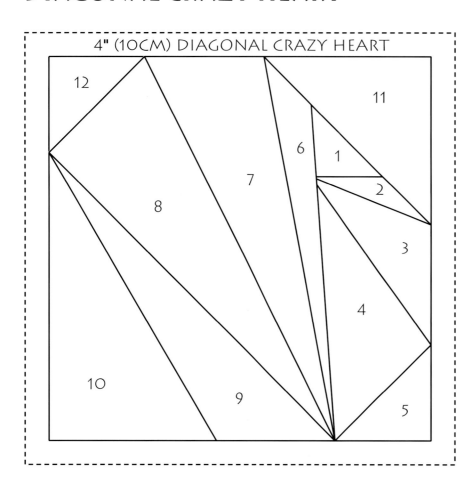

4" (10CM) DIAGONAL CRAZY HEART

12 11 6 1 7 2 8 3 4 10 9 5

DIAGONAL DOUBLE HEART

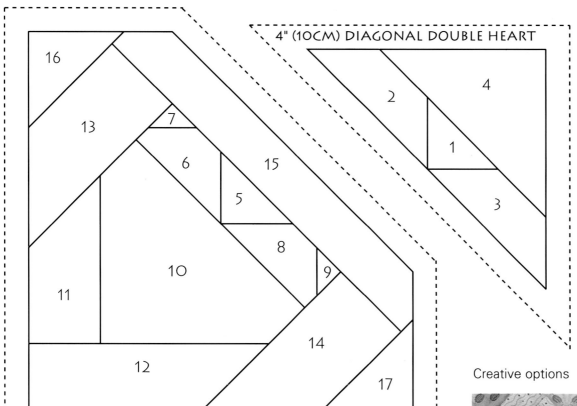

4" (10CM) DIAGONAL DOUBLE HEART

4" (10CM) DIAGONAL DOUBLE HEART

Creative options

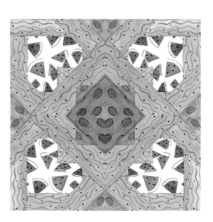

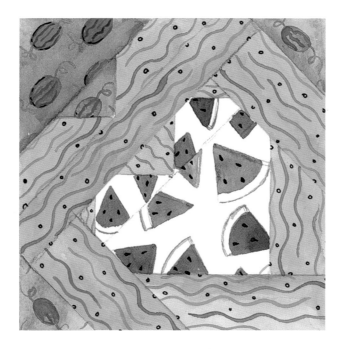

PUZZLE HEART II

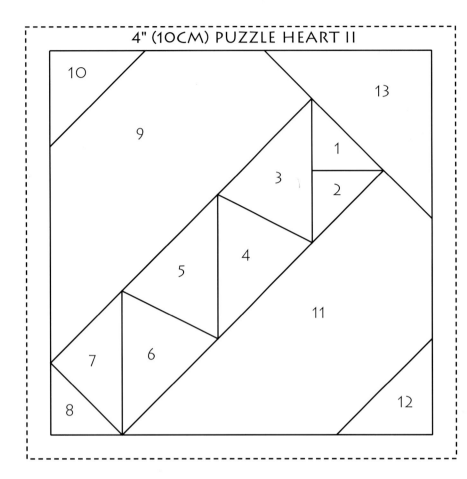

4" (10CM) PUZZLE HEART II

Creative options

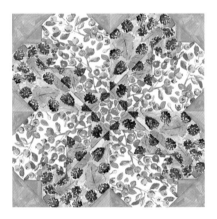

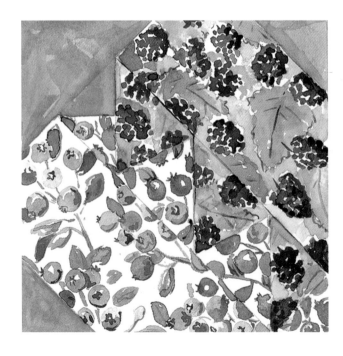

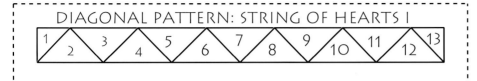

STRING OF HEARTS

(INSERTION PATTERN)

Creative options

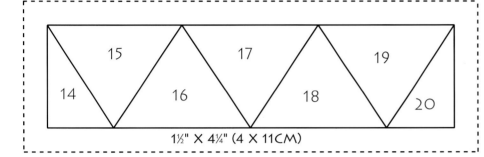

DIAGONAL PATTERN: STRING OF HEARTS I

1 2 3 4 5 6 7 8 9 10 11 12 13

15 17 19

14 16 18 20

1½" X 4¼" (4 X 11CM)

Suggested use in Diagonal Heart Frame (page 45)

FLOWERS AND ANIMAL FRIENDS

Flowers, butterflies, and cuddly animals always conjure up images of romance. Decorate your Valentines with these blocks, or make a sweet sampler for a friend.

FLOWER BASKET ◆

Sash fabrics make this basket special. "Fill" the basket with buttons or yo-yos.

RESURRECTION BUTTERFLY ◆ ◆

Another dramatic butterfly pattern, this one looks striking when made with either Amish or hand-dyed solid fabrics.

LOVE BIRD ◆ ◆

This sweet little bird is adorable and so easy to make. Use a favorite button for the eye.

SCOTTIE DOG ◆ ◆

With a loyal heart, this little dog makes a great accent to a playful quilt.

ROSE IN BLOOM ◆ ◆

Spiraling petals lead your eyes into the heart of this flower. Varying patterns and colors will help make your own special rose garden.

PLAYFUL KITTY ◆ ◆

Every cat lover knows the joy that a frisky, furry friend can bring. Make this quilt for that special cat lover in your life.

FUCHSIA ◆ ◆

Bright with color, the fuchsia blossom dazzles the eye. Let this pattern sizzle in your fabric garden.

FANTASY VINE ◆ ◆

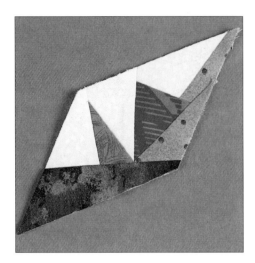

A series of these vine blocks can be arranged into any layout that works with diamond shapes.

BUD AND BUTTERFLY ◆ ◆

Another traditional pattern, this block offers many color possibilities. Enjoy making butterflies flit around a garden of flowers.

HIDDEN FLOWER ◆ ◆

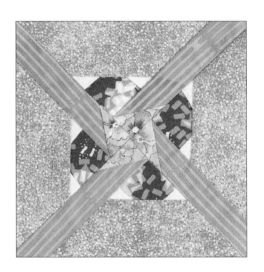

This is an adaptation of a traditional pattern with many different coloring possibilities. The resulting quilt's overall design will be full of energy and diagonal movement.

BUTTERFLY III ◆ ◆ ◆

This fragile creature will grace your next flower garden in fabric.

ORIENTAL TULIP ◆ ◆ ◆

This stalwart flower can brighten your fabric gardens and carry your thoughts of love in a permanent display.

BASKET OF FLOWERS ◆ ◆ ◆

This traditional block is striking when made in contemporary fabrics. Send a small basket of cheerful flowers to a friend!

BROMELIAD FLOWER ◆ ◆ ◆

Full of spikes and bright colors, this block is easy to make and requires no seam matching to be brilliant.

FLOWER BASKET

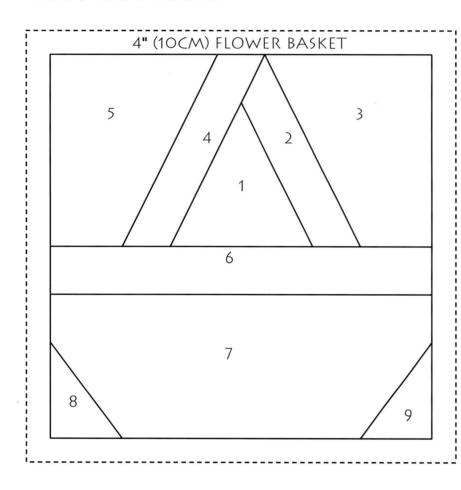

4" (10CM) FLOWER BASKET

5

4

3

2

1

6

7

8

9

Creative options

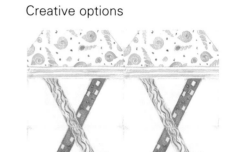

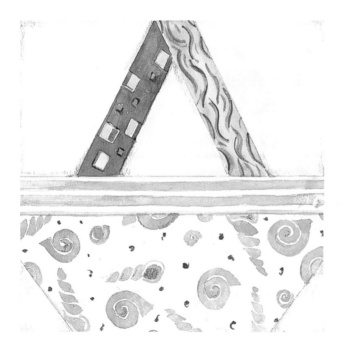

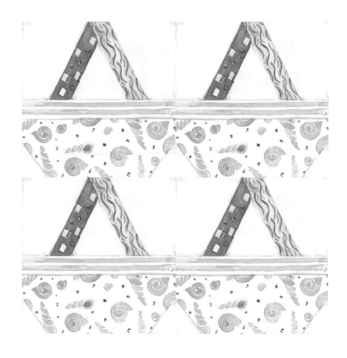

RESURRECTION BUTTERFLY

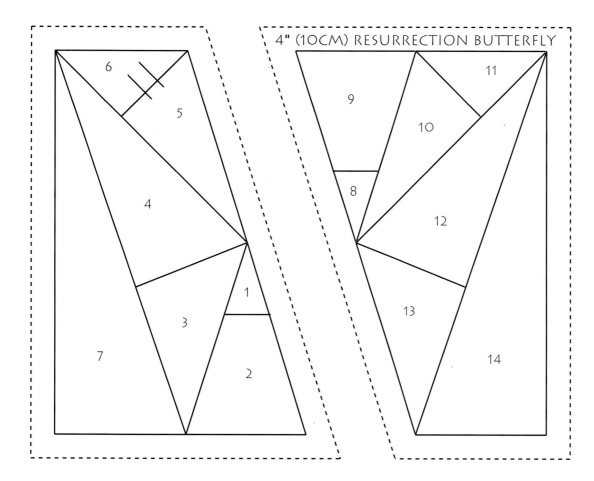

4" (10CM) RESURRECTION BUTTERFLY

PREJOIN THE FABRICS FOR PIECES 5 AND 6; ALIGN THE SEAM, JOINING THESE FABRICS WITH THE SEAM LINE BETWEEN 5 AND 6, THEN SEW THE ENTIRE SEAM JOINING 5/6 TO PIECE 4.

Creative option

LOVE BIRD

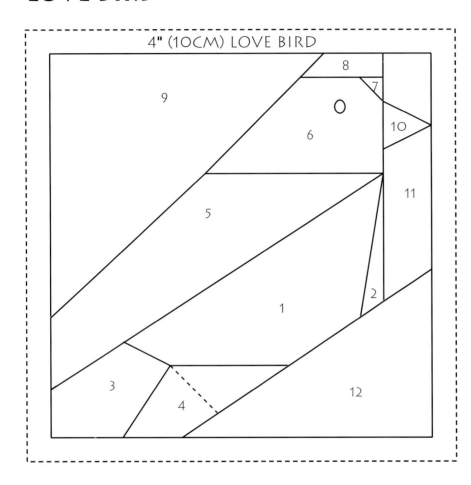

4" (10CM) LOVE BIRD

EYE CAN BE BUTTON OR EMBROIDERY. BEAK SHOULD BE ADDED AS SEPARATE FOLDED 1" (2.5CM) SQUARE (SEWN INTO SEAM WITH PIECE 11). DOTTED LINE SHOWS FOLD LINE FOR PIECE 4 AFTER SEWING.

NOTE: TO SEW PIECE 4, SEE PAGE 19 FOR "STITCH AND TUCK TRICK."

Creative options

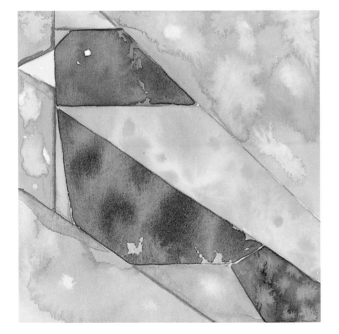

SCOTTIE DOG

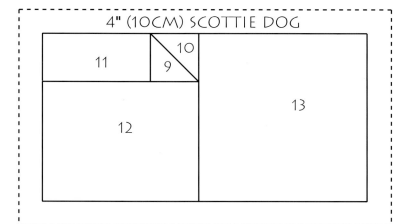

4" (10CM) SCOTTIE DOG

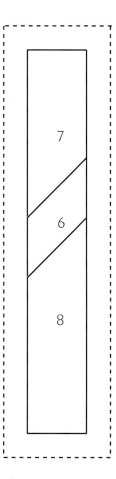

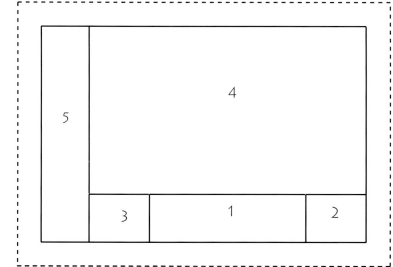

Creative option

PLAYFUL KITTY

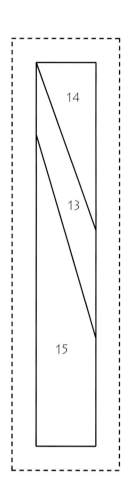

4" (10CM) PLAYFUL KITTY

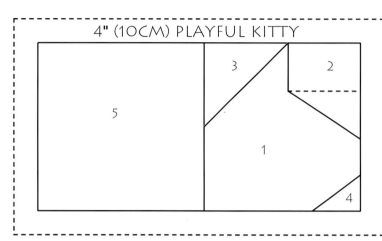

NOTE: TO SEW PIECE 4, SEE PAGE 19 FOR "STITCH AND TUCK TRICK."

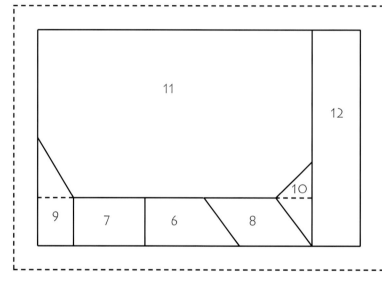

Creative option

ROSE IN BLOOM

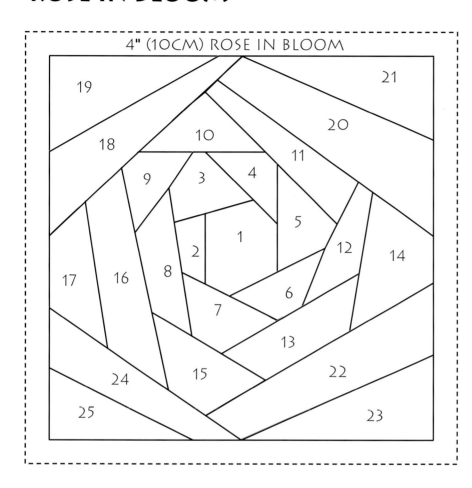

4" (10CM) ROSE IN BLOOM

19

21

18

10

20

9

3

4

11

5

1

2

12

14

8

17

16

6

7

13

24

15

22

25

23

Creative option

FUCHSIA

4" (10CM) FUCHSIA

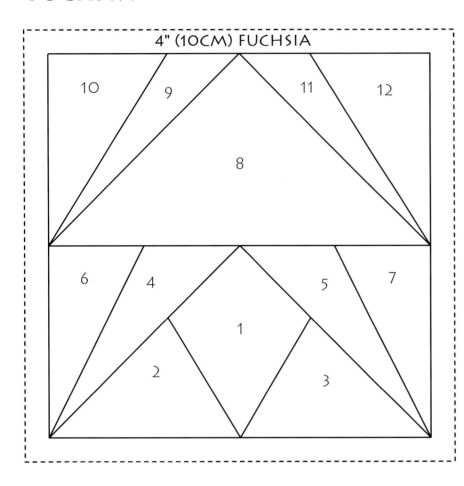

Creative options

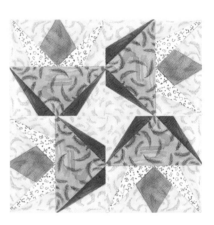

FANTASY VINE

FANTASY VINE

2½" X 3" (6.5 X 7.5CM)

Creative options

BUD AND BUTTERFLY

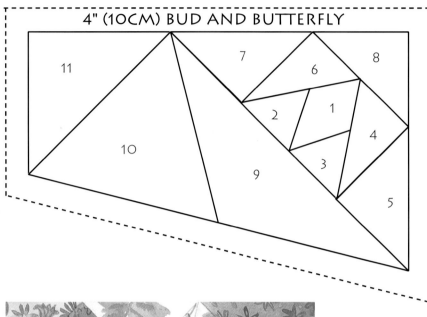

4" (10CM) BUD AND BUTTERFLY

Creative options

HIDDEN FLOWER

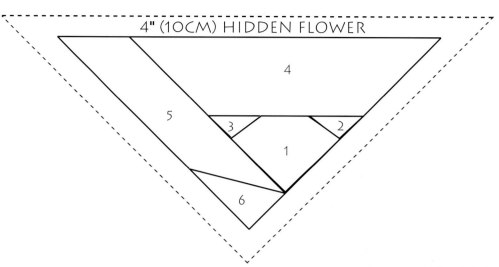

4" (10CM) HIDDEN FLOWER

Creative options

BUTTERFLY III

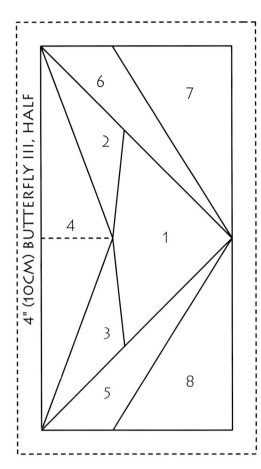

4" (10CM) BUTTERFLY III, HALF

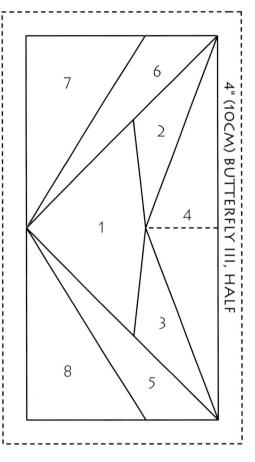

4" (10CM) BUTTERFLY III, HALF

INSERT A PIECE OF BLACK PIPING BETWEEN SEAMS FOR BODY. (OPTIONAL) NOTE: TO SEW PIECE 4, SEE PAGE 19 FOR "STITCH AND TUCK TRICK."

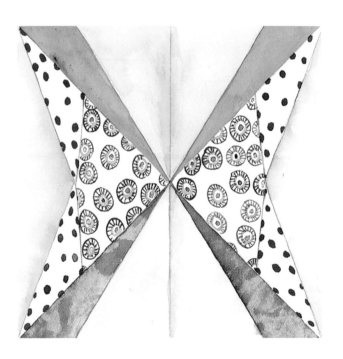

Creative option

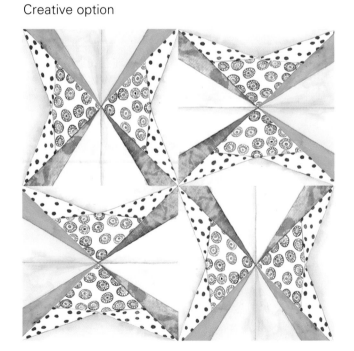

ORIENTAL TULIP

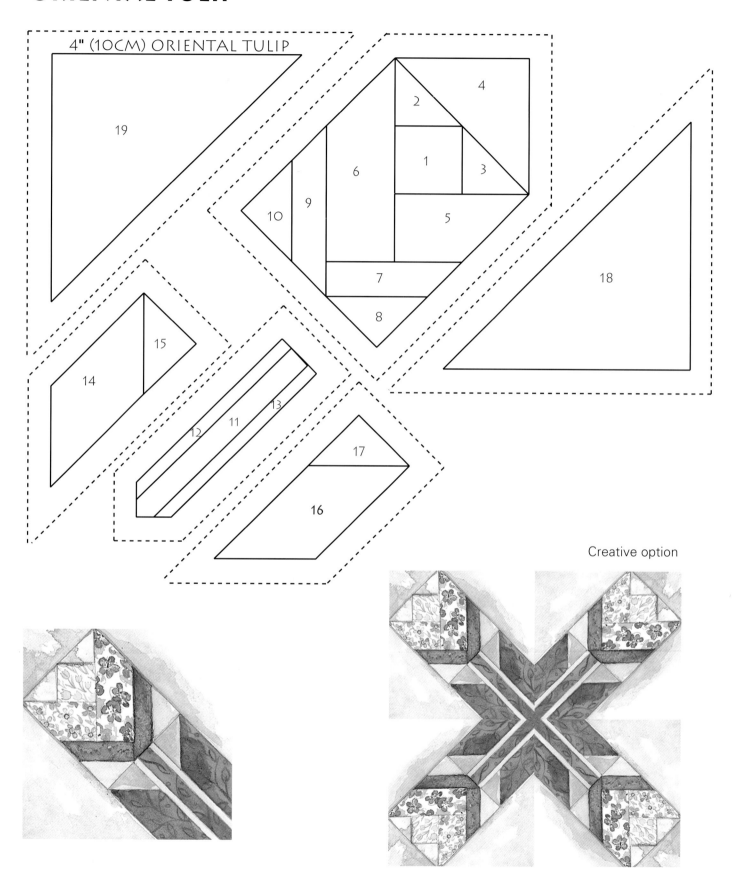

4" (10CM) ORIENTAL TULIP

19

4

2

1

3

6

9

10

5

7

8

18

15

14

13

12 11

17

16

Creative option

BROMELIAD FLOWER

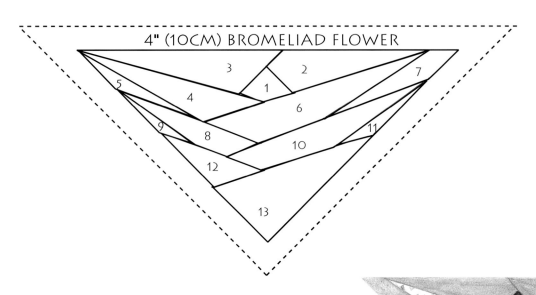

4" (10CM) BROMELIAD FLOWER

Creative options

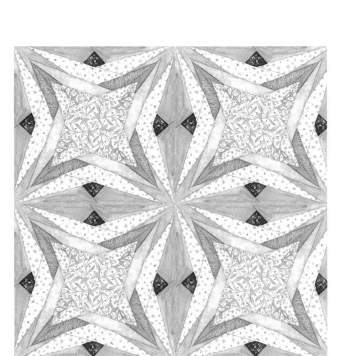

BASKET OF FLOWERS

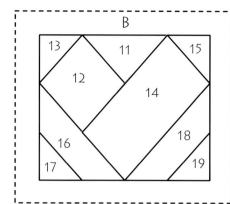

B
13 11 15
12
14
16
18
17 19

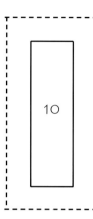

10

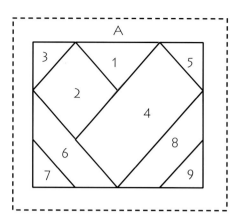

A
3 1 5
2
4
6 8
7 9

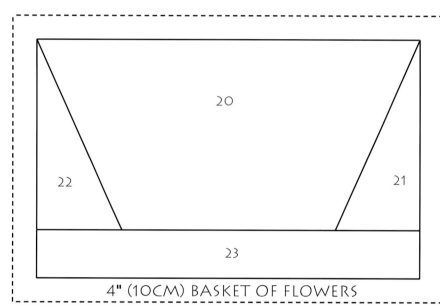

20

22 21

23

4" (10CM) BASKET OF FLOWERS

Creative option

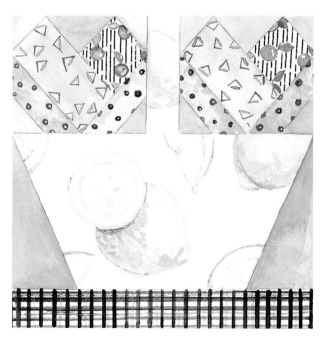

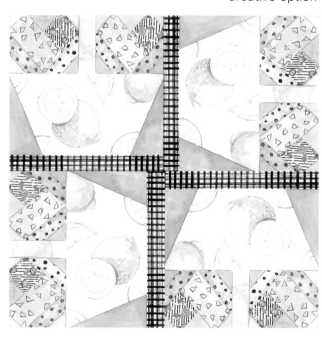

HANDS OF LOVE

The touch of a hand in friendship and affection speaks as loudly as words to the heart. Weave these patterns into your fabric messages.

TESSELLATING HANDS ♦ ♦

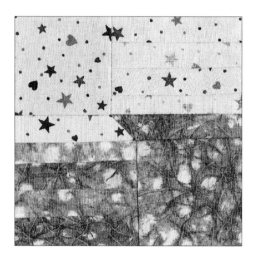

Repeat this pattern over and over to make a wonderful quilt design. Consider using many colors for the hands to express teamwork and community.

HEART IN HAND ♦ ♦ ♦

This block serves well as an explicit Valentine offering your heart to the one you love.

DIAGONAL HEART IN HAND ♦ ♦ ♦

Use this pattern for a corner setting in a heart quilt for your loved one.

HANDS OF FRIENDSHIP ♦ ♦ ♦

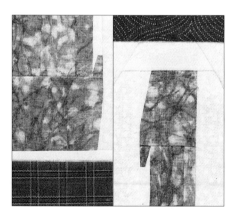

Extend a hand in friendship or an offer of love with this block pattern.

TESSELLATING HANDS

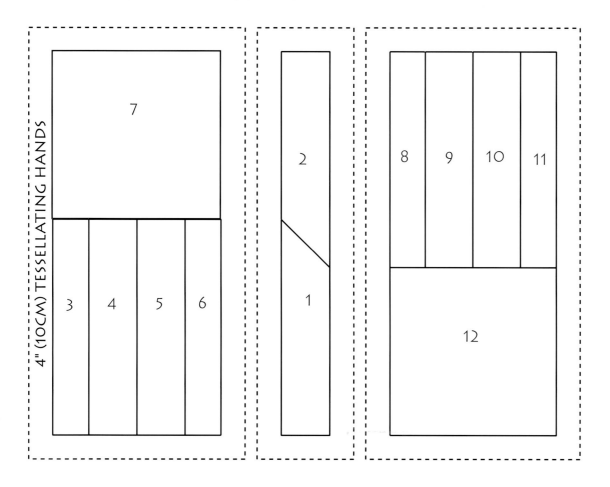

4" (10CM) TESSELLATING HANDS

Creative option

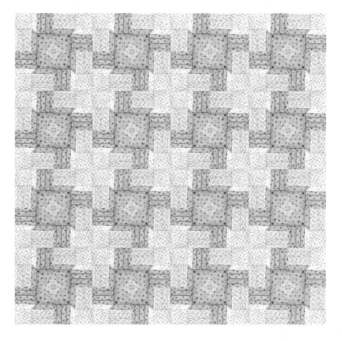

HEART IN HAND

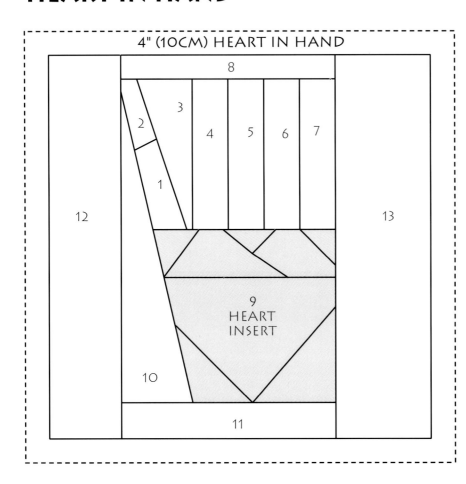

4" (10CM) HEART IN HAND

8
3
2
4 5 6 7
1
12 13
9
HEART
INSERT
10
11

HEART INSERT

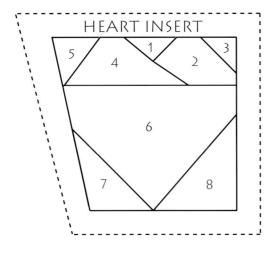

5 1 3
4 2
6
7 8

Creative options

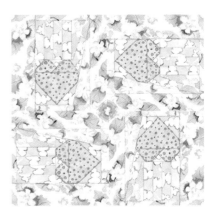

DIAGONAL HEART IN HAND

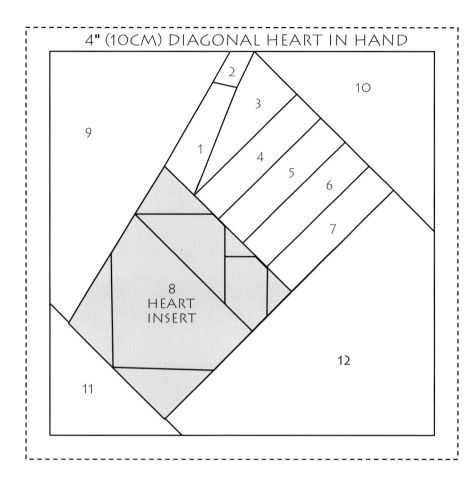

4" (10CM) DIAGONAL HEART IN HAND

Creative options

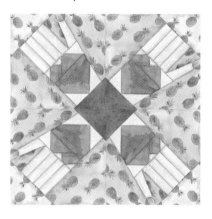

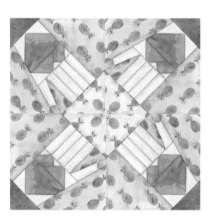

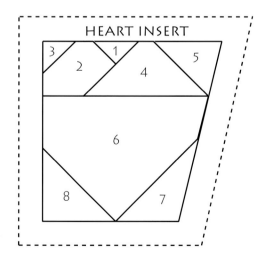

HEART INSERT

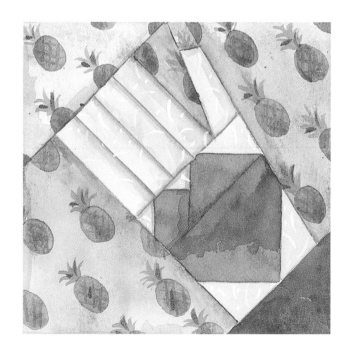

HANDS OF FRIENDSHIP

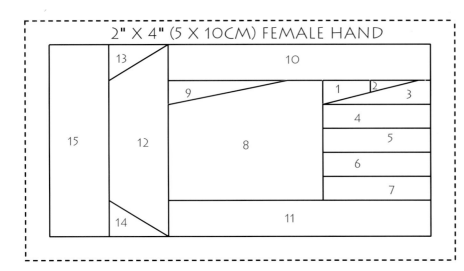

2" X 4" (5 X 10CM) FEMALE HAND

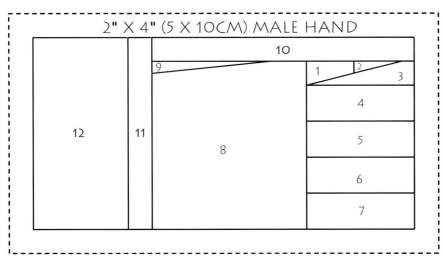

2" X 4" (5 X 10CM) MALE HAND

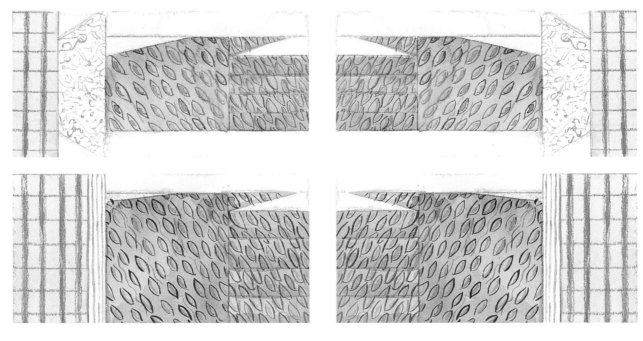

TEA PARTIES AND PICNICS

What's more romantic than an afternoon outing? Whether it's a fancy tea party or a breezy summer picnic, these blocks will help you make a fabric occasion to cherish.

ICE CREAM CONE ◆

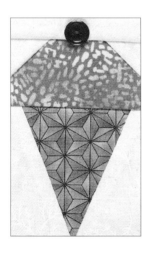

Ice cream is a sweet treat to share with friends or lovers, and this delicious block will surely add a nice touch to a special friendship quilt.

ICE CREAM SUNDAE ◆

Share a sundae with a special friend, or make a whole quilt full of flavors for that calorie-free treat.

TEA PARTY DELIGHTS ◆

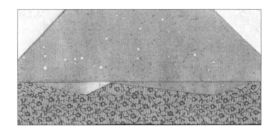

Cupcakes and tea cake make special party fare. Enjoy them in your favorite fabric tea party.

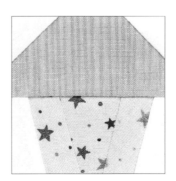

PICNIC BASKET ◆

Pack up this basket and add some treats to remember a favorite outing or start a new tradition.

FRIENDSHIP MUG ◆ ◆

Make a whole cupboard full of special mugs for your kitchen.

FRIENDSHIP MUG WITH HEART ◆ ◆

The design of this mug expresses your feelings for good friends or Valentines.

CUP AND SAUCER ◆ ◆

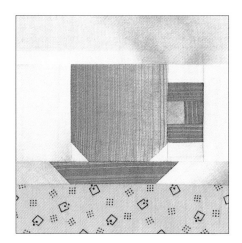

Clinking porcelain sounds so sweet when accompanied by a friend's laughter. Have fun choosing wild prints for a fancy collection of these charming sets.

COFFEE POT ◆ ◆ ◆

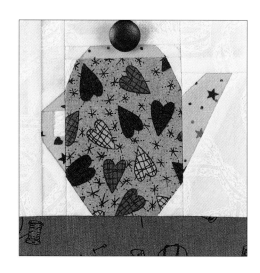

Remember that special coffee pot Grandma used when you were a child? Recapture that warm memory with this block.

TEAPOT ◆ ◆ ◆

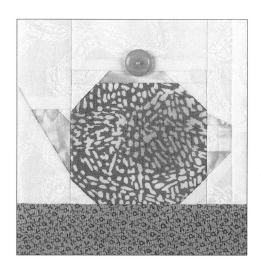

What could be more pleasant than spending an afternoon over a warm pot of steaming tea—call in your friends and enjoy!

ICE CREAM CONE

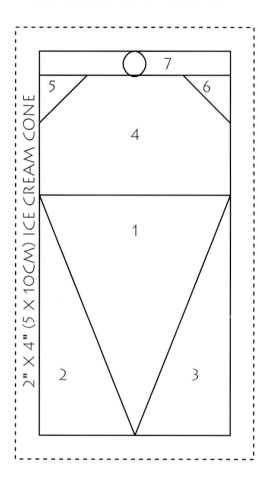

USE 1/4" (6MM) OR 3/8" (1CM) BUTTON FOR CHERRY.

ICE CREAM SUNDAE

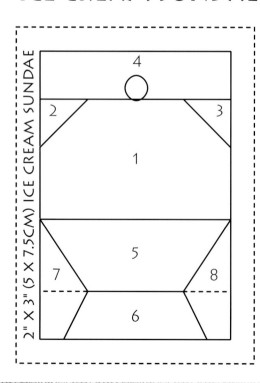

CHERRY CAN BE A 1/4" (6MM) OR 3/8" (1CM) BUTTON; DASHED INTERNAL LINES DENOTE FOLD/TUCK IN FABRIC OF PIECES 7 AND 8.

NOTE: TO SEW PIECES 7 AND 8, SEE PAGE 19 FOR "STITCH AND TUCK TRICK."

TEA PARTY DELIGHTS

2" (5CM) CUPCAKE

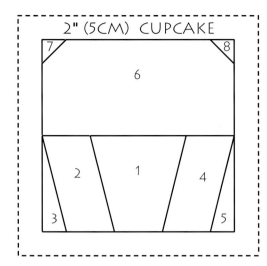

2" X 4" (5 X 10CM) TEA CAKE

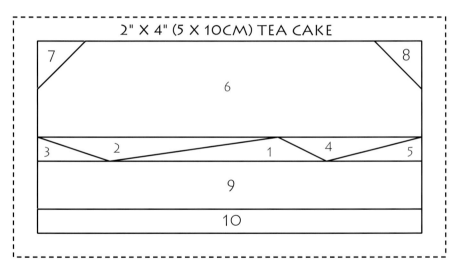

PICNIC BASKET

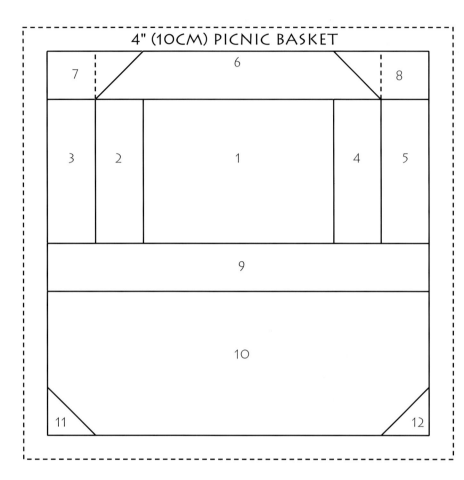

4" (10CM) PICNIC BASKET

| 7 | 6 | 8 |

| 3 | 2 | 1 | 4 | 5 |

9

10

11 | 12

DOTTED LINES SHOW FOLD LINE FOR PIECES 7 AND 8, AFTER SEWING.

NOTE: TO SEW PIECES 7 AND 8, SEE PAGE 19 FOR "STITCH AND TUCK TRICK."

Creative options

FRIENDSHIP MUG

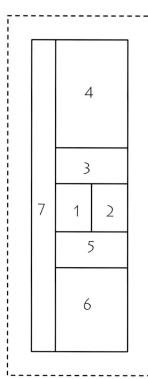

4" (10CM) FRIENDSHIP MUG

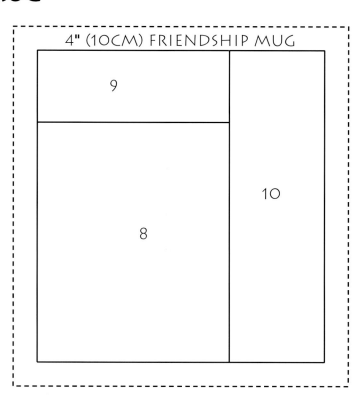

11

Creative option

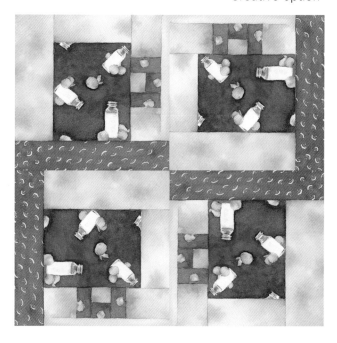

FRIENDSHIP MUG WITH HEART

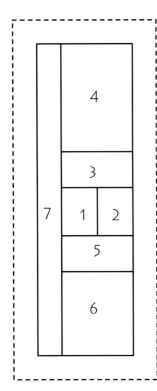

4" (10CM) FRIENDSHIP MUG WITH HEART

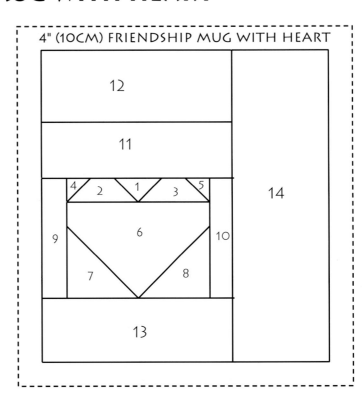

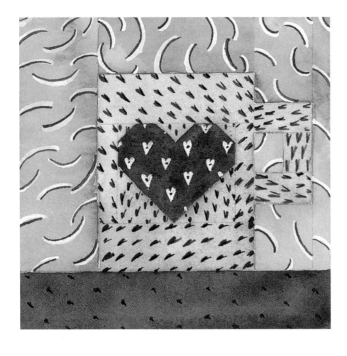

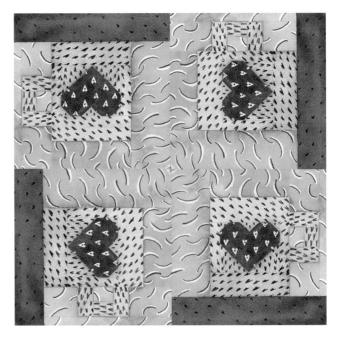

Creative option

CUP AND SAUCER

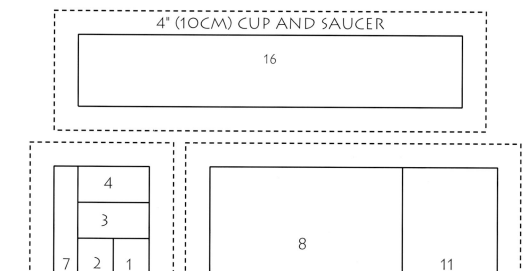

4" (10CM) CUP AND SAUCER

16

7	4		
	3		
	2	1	
	5		
	6		

8 11

9 10

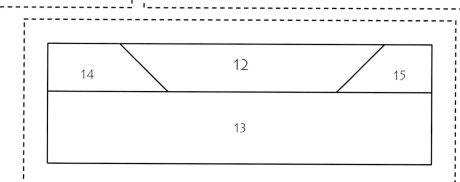

14   12   15

13

Creative option

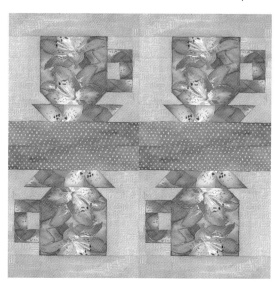

COFFEE POT

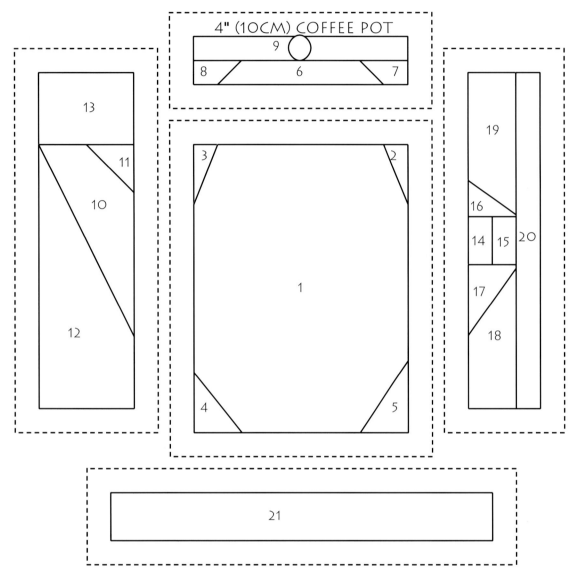

4" (10CM) COFFEE POT

9

8   6   7

13

11

10

12

3   2

1

4   5

19

16

14 15 20

17

18

21

CHOOSE A
1/4" (6MM)
OR 3/8" (1CM)
BUTTON
FOR COFFEE
POT TOPPER.
YOU MAY
CHOOSE TO
COVER YOUR
BUTTON IN
A FABRIC
THAT
MATCHES
YOUR
COFFEE POT.

Creative option

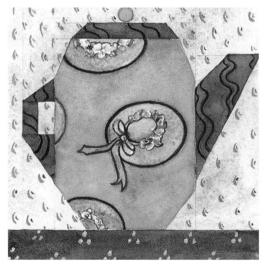

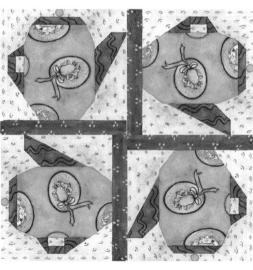

TEAPOT

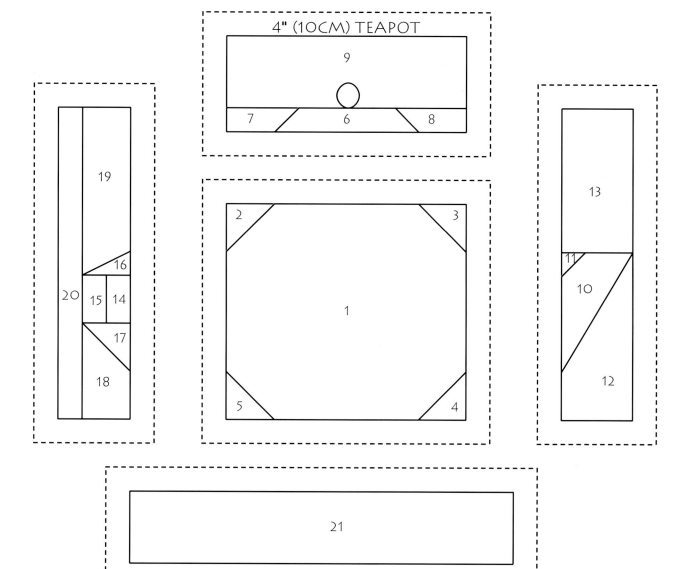

4" (10CM) TEAPOT

CHOOSE A 1/4"
(6MM) OR 3/8"
(1CM) BUTTON
FOR TEAPOT
TOPPER. YOU
MAY CHOOSE
TO COVER
YOUR BUTTON
IN A FABRIC
THAT MATCHES
YOUR TEAPOT.

Creative option

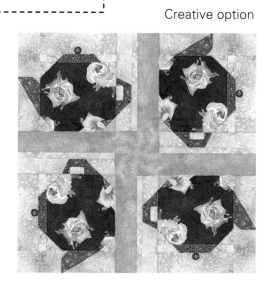

SPECIAL VALENTINES

These blocks are inspired by one of the most magical experiences—being in love. Share these with the special person in your life.

CUPID'S ARROW ◆

(INSERTION PATTERN)

The quick dart of love strikes many an unsuspecting person. Send your loving wishes with this Valentine insert block.

FALLING IN LOVE ◆ ◆ ◆

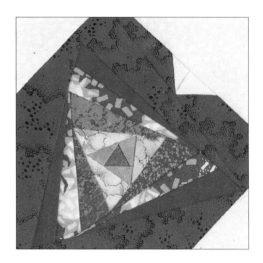

Capture all the excitement of that dizzying experience of being in love with this block.

LOVE ◆ ◆ ◆

(INSERTION PATTERN)

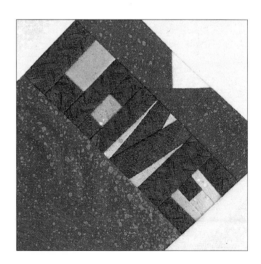

You can clearly spell out your feelings for your most special Valentine with this block.

SWEET NOTHINGS ◆ ◆

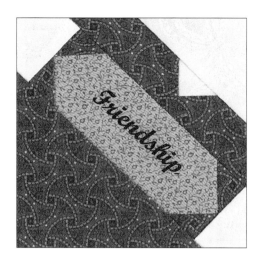

Remember those candy hearts with Valentine messages we ate as children? Make your own here.
Rubber-stamp or letter your thoughts to a friend or
loved one right onto this block and re-create that
childhood fun!

LOVE AT HOME ◆ ◆ ◆
(INSERTION PATTERN)

This house is brimming with love, capturing the feel-
ing of love at home. Make one for your next quilt.

WRAPPED IN LOVE ◆ ◆ ◆
(INSERTION PATTERN)

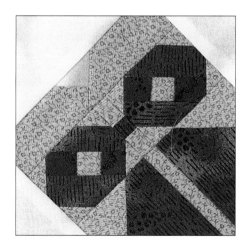

Wrap up your love with a special bow using this
pattern.

CUPID'S ARROW

(INSERTION PATTERN)

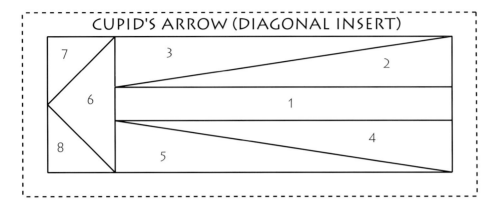

CUPID'S ARROW (DIAGONAL INSERT)

7
3
2
6
1
8
4
5

Creative options

FALLING IN LOVE

4" (10CM) FALLING IN LOVE

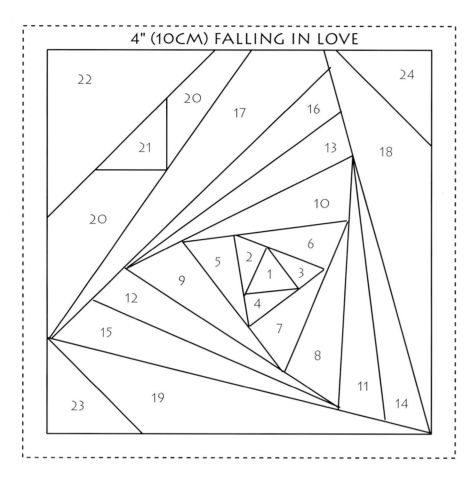

SEW THE TWO 20 PIECES AS ONE STRIP. AFTER SEWING PIECE 21, FOLD ALONG DOTTED LINE TO PRESS UPWARD.

NOTE: TO SEW PIECE 21, SEE PAGE 19 FOR "STITCH AND TUCK TRICK."

Creative options

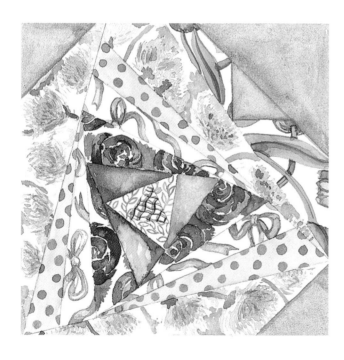

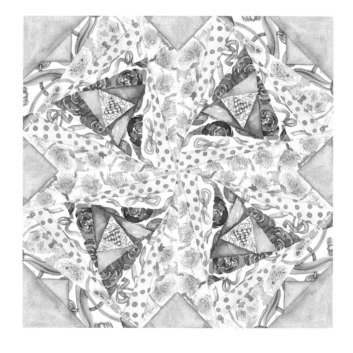

LOVE
(INSERTION PATTERN)

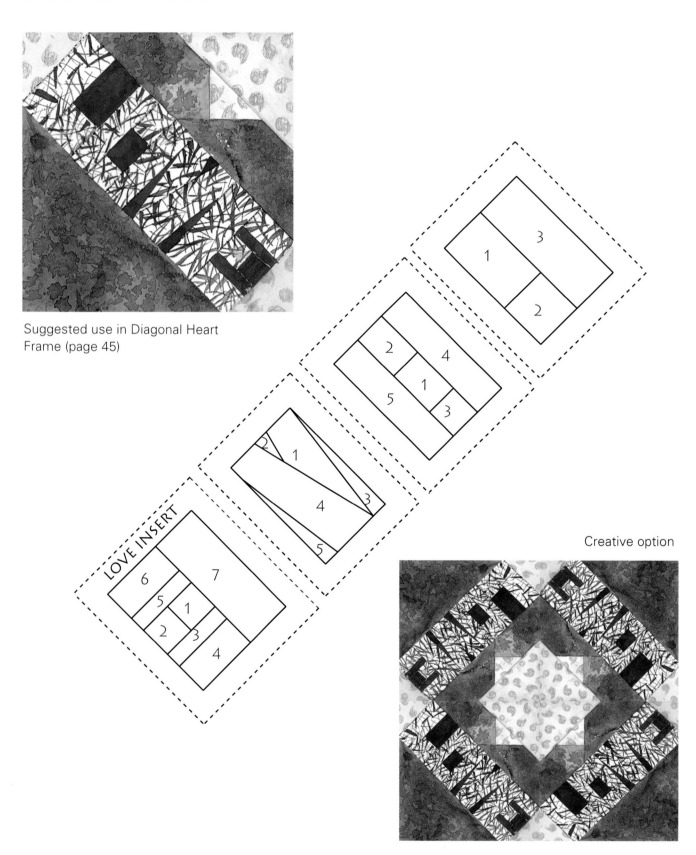

Suggested use in Diagonal Heart
Frame (page 45)

Creative option

SWEET NOTHINGS

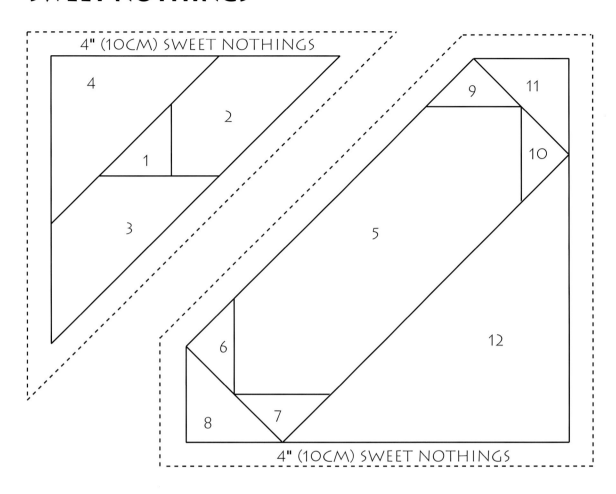

4" (10CM) SWEET NOTHINGS

4

2

1

3

9

11

10

5

6

12

8

7

4" (10CM) SWEET NOTHINGS

Creative option

WRAPPED IN LOVE
(INSERTION PATTERN)

FOR USE WITH DIAGONAL HEART FRAME PATTERN ON PAGE 50. USE MODIFIED PIECE BELOW.

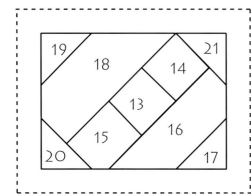

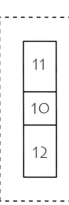

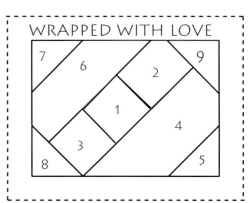

WRAPPED WITH LOVE

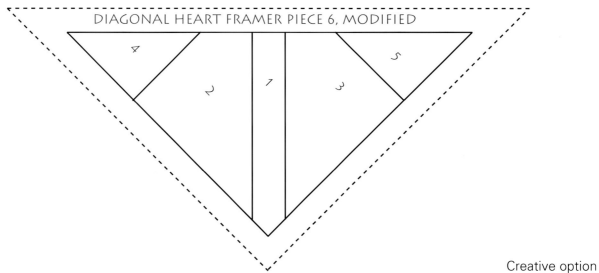

DIAGONAL HEART FRAMER PIECE 6, MODIFIED

Creative option

LOVE AT HOME

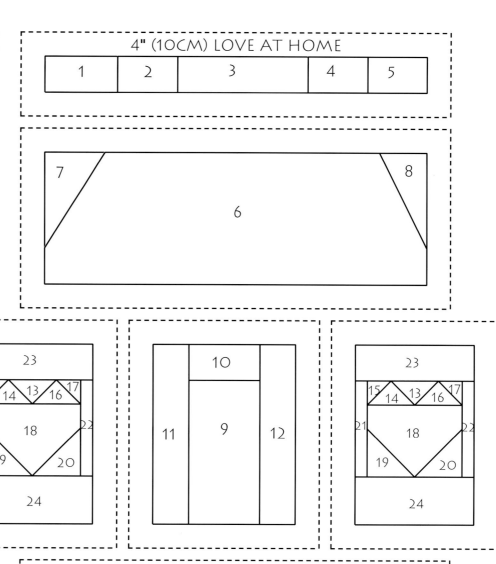

4" (10CM) LOVE AT HOME

| 1 | 2 | 3 | 4 | 5 |

7   6   8

23			23
15 14 13 16 17	10	15 14 13 16 17
21 18 22	11 9 12	21 18 22
19 20		19 20
24		24

25

Creative option

BORDERS

Here are five border patterns that will add the perfect finish to your quilted Valentines. Don't overlook using them as quilt medallions.

CUPID'S DART BORDER ◆

This is an easy pattern and a great way to finish off even a single block to make it ever so special. Enjoy playing with the layout alternatives.

STRING OF HEARTS BORDER ◆ ◆

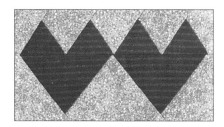

This border is modular in 2" (5cm) hearts and will work well for many quilts. The hearts can be made of many scraps or of a single fabric at your whim.

TINY HEARTS BORDER ◆ ◆

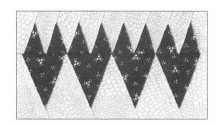

These spiky little hearts are chock-full of energy. Use this pattern to border a special quilt and finish it with vigor.

TESSELLATING STRING OF HEARTS BORDER ◆ ◆

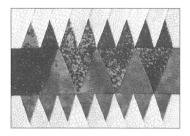

This pattern takes a bit more time, but the results are splendid!

TESSELLATING TINY HEARTS BORDER ◆ ◆

This frame will give your quilt an extra dose of excitement.

CUPID'S DART BORDER

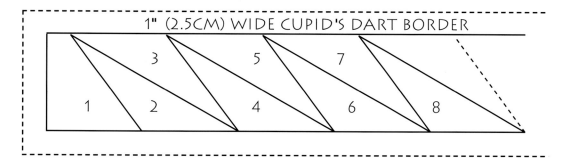

1" (2.5CM) WIDE CUPID'S DART BORDER

3   5   7

1   2   4   6   8

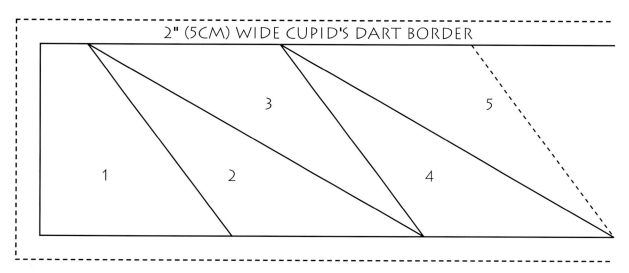

2" (5CM) WIDE CUPID'S DART BORDER

3   5

1   2   4

Creative options

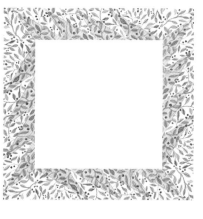

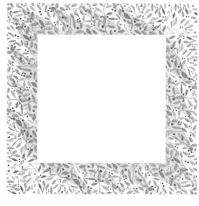

STRING OF HEARTS BORDER

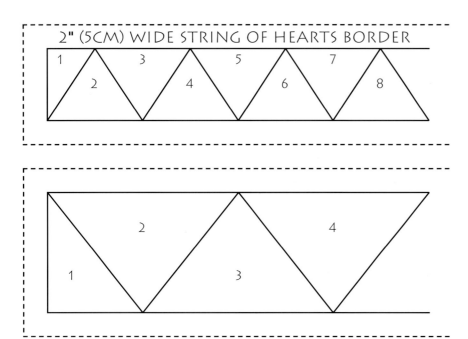

2" (5CM) WIDE STRING OF HEARTS BORDER

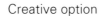

Creative option

TINY HEARTS BORDER

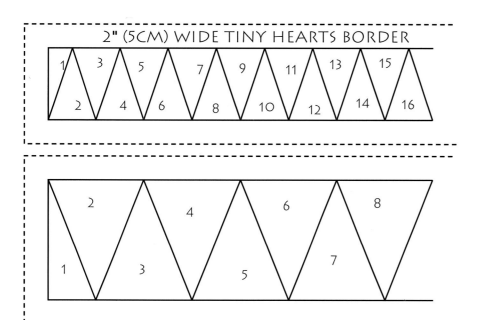

2" (5CM) WIDE TINY HEARTS BORDER

1 3 5 7 9 11 13 15

2 4 6 8 10 12 14 16

2 4 6 8

1 3 5 7

Creative options

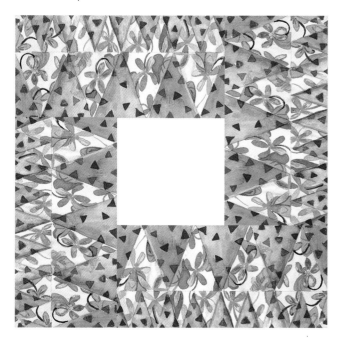

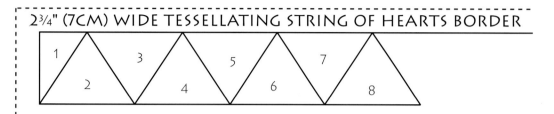

TESSELLATING STRING OF HEARTS BORDER

2¾" (7CM) WIDE TESSELLATING STRING OF HEARTS BORDER

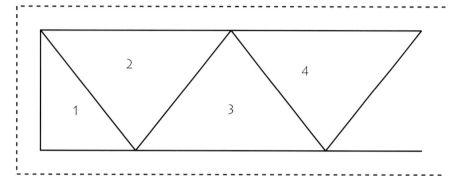

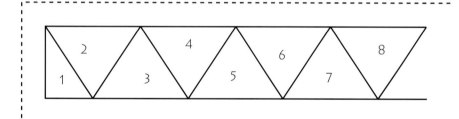

Creative options

TESSELLATING TINY HEARTS BORDER

2³⁄₄" (7CM) WIDE TESSELLATING TINY HEARTS BORDER

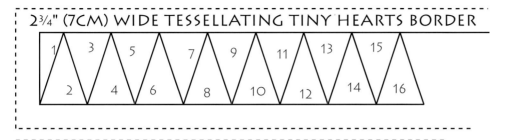

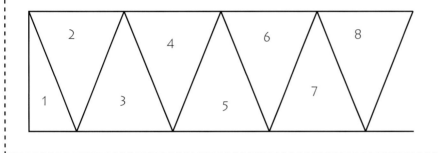

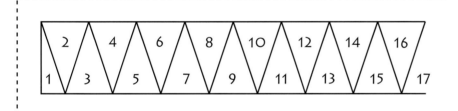

Creative options

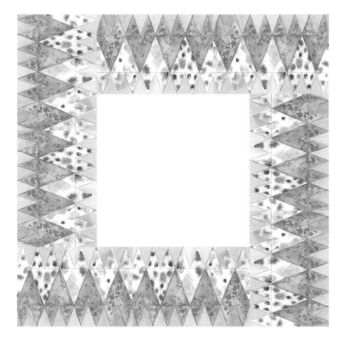
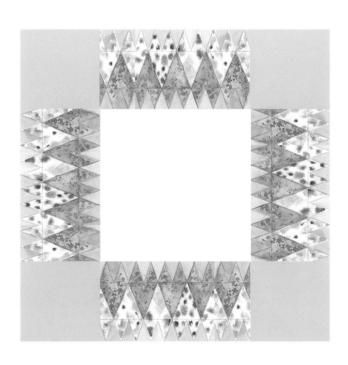

♦ CHAPTER THREE ♦

QUILT AND ACCESSORY DESIGNS

QUILT AND ACCESSORY DESIGNS

Here are 5 miniature quilt designs and a Valentine design, each using one or more of the quilt blocks in this book. Use these projects as a starting point for your journey into foundation piecing. An easy way to begin is to choose nine blocks, make them up in coordinating fabrics, then stitch them together to make a sampler quilt. This is a great way to try several block designs and gain proficiency at foundation piecing at the same time.

Foundation piecing needn't be limited to miniature quilts. You can enlarge the blocks to make a full-size quilt of 8" (20cm) blocks (see page 15); for a larger quilt, add more blocks to the design.

Besides its simplicity, one of the beauties of foundation piecing is the opportunity it presents to use small amounts of leftover fabrics—a scrap saver's dream come true! The quilts shown here generally require less than one-quarter yard (23cm) of any one fabric; most use much less.

Linda's quilts show just a few of the many ways each of the quilt designs can be used. From scrap quilts comprised of dozens of fabrics to two-color quilts, the possibilities for interpreting these designs are endless. The fabrics Linda has chosen for the quilts are only suggestions. Make these quilts your own by choosing your favorite colors.

Many of the quilts would be perfect in a Valentine color combination of red and white. For dimension, add a little pink. You can go a little fur-ther still and add a touch of soft green for just the right contrast.

Combine stripes, plaids, prints, and solids for interesting blocks full of movement and surprise. Or redesign any of the quilts. You can rework the Puppy Love quilt by substituting the Love Bird block for the Kitty and Puppy blocks.

To test your fabric choices for a quilt design, piece a block or glue fabric to a copy of each block design and make color copies. You can then put these together to see exactly what the quilt will look like before you stitch the remaining blocks. Mix and match any three block designs for the fabric Valentines.

Fabric requirements are specified for all of the quilts and the bonus accessories. These represent the amounts Linda used. Fabric usage can vary depending upon cutting efficiency, so be sure to purchase a little extra fabric. Remaining yardage can be used as binding or pieced together for interesting quilt backings.

HEARTTHROB

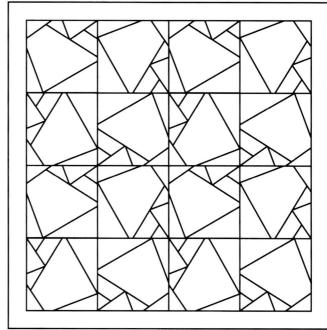

FINISHED SIZE: 24" x 24" (61 x 61cm)

FABRIC REQUIREMENTS:
    BLOCKS: Large scraps of three different fabrics
    INNER BORDER: Two strips 1½" x 16½"
        (4 x 42cm) and two strips 1½" x 18½"
        (4 x 47cm)
    OUTER BORDER: Two strips 3½" x 18½"
        (9 x 47cm) and two strips 3½" x 24½"
        (9 x 62cm)
    BACKING: 28" x 28" (71 x 71cm)
    BATTING: 24" x 24" (61 x 61cm)

HEARTTHROB BLOCK (Page 43)
    4" (10cm) block size
    Make 8

PUPPY LOVE

FINISHED SIZE: 8" x 26" (20.5 x 66cm)

FABRIC REQUIREMENTS:

    BLOCKS: Assorted fabrics

    BORDER: Five 4½" x 2½" (11.5 x 6.5cm)
        pieces to go between and to both sides of
        the blocks and two 26½" x 2½" (21 x 6.5cm)
        pieces for top and bottom border

    BACKING: 12" x 30" (30.5 x 76cm)

    BATTING: 12" x 30" (30.5 x 76cm)

SCOTTIE DOG BLOCK (Page 59)

    4" (10cm) block size

    Make 1

PLAYFUL KITTEN BLOCK (Page 60)

    4" (10cm) block size

    Make 1

FLOWER BASKET (Page 56)

    4" (10cm) block size

    Make 1

GARDEN FLUTTER

FINISHED SIZE: 11" x 11" (28 x 28cm)

FABRIC REQUIREMENTS:
    BLOCKS: Assorted fabrics
    BORDER: Assorted fabrics
    BACKING: 14" x 14" (35.5 x 35.5cm)
    BATTING: 14" x 14" (35.5 x 35.5cm)
    BINDING: 1¾" (4.5cm) wide strips

BUD AND BUTTERFLY (Page 64)
    4" (10cm) block size
    Make 4
    Stitch 1" (2.5cm) wide solid color fabric strips to
        outside edges of assembled quilt blocks.

CUPID'S DART BORDER (Page 95)
    1" (2.5cm) wide border
    Make 4 (pattern and mirror flip to make one
        border.)

AFTERNOON DELIGHT

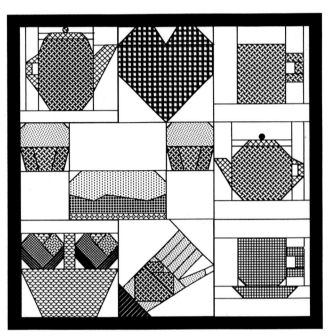

FINISHED SIZE: 13" x 13" (33 x 33cm)

FABRIC REQUIREMENTS: Scraps of fabric
BLOCKS: Two 2½" (6.5cm) squares to add to the Cupcake blocks
One 2½" x 4½" (6 x 11cm) rectangle to add to the Tea Cake block
BORDER: 1" (2.5cm) wide strips to finish ½" (1.3cm) wide
BACKING: 16" x 16" (40.5 x 40.5cm)
BATTING: 16" x 16" (40.5 x 40.5cm)
BINDING: 1¾" (4.5cm) wide strips

CUPCAKE (Page 79)
2" (5cm) block size
Make 2

COFFEE POT (Page 84)
4" (10cm) block size
Make 1

LARGE UPRIGHT HEART (Page 28)
4" (10cm) block size
Make 1

FRIENDSHIP MUG (Page 81)
4" (10cm) block size
Make 1

TEA CAKE (Page 79)
2" x 4" (5 x 10cm) block size
Make 1

TEAPOT (Page 85)
4" (10cm) block size
Make 1

BASKET OF FLOWERS (Page 69)
4" (10cm) block size
Make 1

DIAGONAL HEART IN HAND (Page 73)
4" (10cm) block size
Make 1

CUP AND SAUCER (Page 83)
4" (10cm) block size
Make 1

A CELEBRATION BANNER

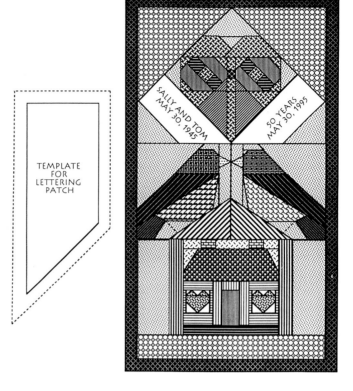

TEMPLATE FOR LETTERING PATCH

FINISHED SIZE: 9" x 16" (22 x 40.5cm)

FABRIC REQUIREMENTS:

  BLOCKS: Assorted fabrics
  BORDER: 1" (2.5cm) wide strips to finish ½" (1.3cm)
  BACKING: 12" x 19" (30 x 48cm)
  BATTING: 12" x 19" (30 x 48cm)
  BINDING: 1¾" (4.5cm) wide strips

WRAPPED IN LOVE INSERTION PATTERN (Page 92)

  4" (10cm) block size
  Make 1

LOVE BIRD (Page 58)

  4" (10cm) block size
  Make 2, reversing 1

LOVE AT HOME (Page 93)

  4" (10cm) block size
  Make 1

FOR TOP SECTION: Enlarge template to 200 percent. Use the template to cut 2 pieces of light-colored fabric for lettering. Reverse the template for one of the pieces. For upper triangles cut a 4⅞" (12cm) square in half diagonally. For the small corner triangles cut a 2⅝" (6.5cm) square in half diagonally.

FOR THE HOUSE SECTION: Cut 2 pieces, each 1⅛" x 4½" (3 x 11cm), and stitch to the sides of the house blocks. Cut two pieces 1⅞" x 4½" (4.5 x 11cm) to go outside those. For the ground, cut and attach a strip 1½" x 8½" (3.5 x 21.5cm).

Assemble the quilt top and attach the border strips, first to the two sides and then the top and bottom.

VALENTINES

Slip a foundation-pieced Valentine into a fabric envelope for a very special gift. The flap can be secured with a heavy button (no buttonhole necessary), a dangling bead, or a piece of ribbon tied into a bow.

MATERIALS:

Three foundation pieced blocks
1" (2.5cm) wide strip for Valentine border
Backing fabric
Envelope fabric
Envelope fastener as desired

NOTE: All seam allowances are ¼" (6mm) unless specified otherwise.

INSTRUCTIONS

1. **Valentine:** Stitch three pieced blocks together side by side. Stitch the border strips to the sides as shown. Press. Cut a piece of backing fabric 5½" x 13½" (13.5 x 34cm). Right sides together, stitch the assembled blocks/border to the backing, leaving about 1" inch (2.5cm) long opening for turning. Turn right side out. Hand sew the opening closed. Press.

2. **Envelope:** Right sides together, stitch the two envelope pieces, leaving a 2" (5cm) opening along the bottom edge for turning. Trim corners. Turn right side out. Handstitch the opening closed. Press. Attach closure of your choice.

TO MAKE PATTERN, BUTT AND TAPE THE TWO PATTERN PIECES TOGETHER

VALENTINE ENVELOPE, PART II

TO MAKE PATTERN, BUTT AND TAPE TO PART I.

PART II

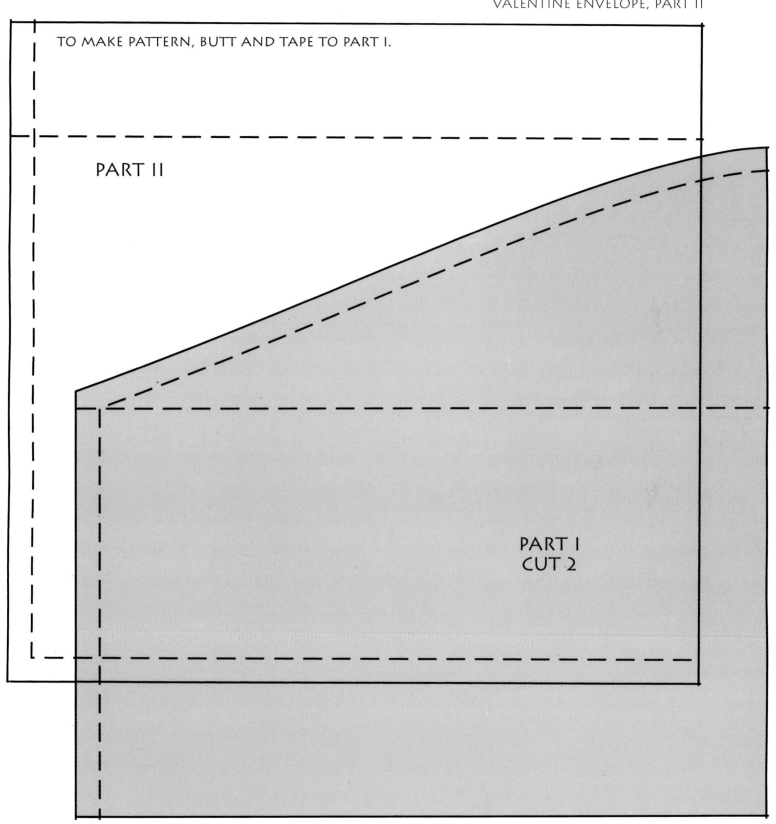

PART I
CUT 2

VALENTINE ENVELOPE, PART I

♦ CHAPTER FOUR ♦

FINISHING

FINISHING

This chapter contains instructions for completing your quilt top, making the quilt "sandwich," binding your quilt, and adding a sleeve for hanging. Refer to the general quilting titles listed in the bibliography for thorough discussions of these topics as well as for excellent books on machine quilting.

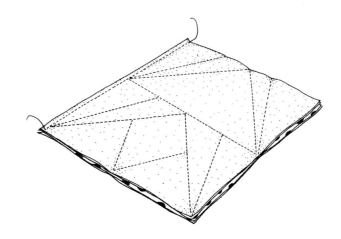

JOINING THE BLOCKS

Lay out the blocks according to the layout diagram for the quilt you are making. Beginning at the top left corner, match the adjoining sides of the first two blocks together, right sides facing. Since pins tend to distort the paper foundations, use a paper clip to hold the match points in place. Baste ¼" (6mm) from the raw edge, as marked on the foundation. Check to make sure seams match and points meet where necessary. Stitch.

Vinyl-coated paper clips are especially good to use as the vinyl protects your fabric from marks that uncoated metal paper clips may leave.

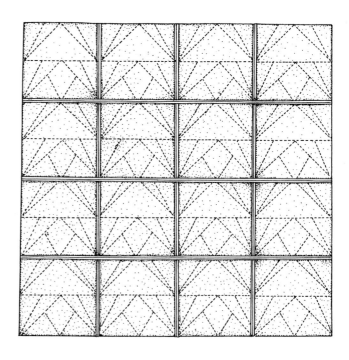

Keep adding blocks until you have completed the top horizontal row. Do the same for each remaining row. Press seam allowances open. Stitch the rows together, carefully matching seams. Press seam allowances open.

NOTE: Some block patterns include strategic points that must match when the rows are stitched. In this case I baste the blocks together, check the alignment, and then stitch when I'm satisfied they match up properly.

REMOVING THE PAPER

If you used paper as the foundation for your quilt, gently tear the paper from the backs of the blocks now, as if you were tearing stamps. Press the blocks gently, lifting the iron up and down rather than dragging it, so as not to distort the blocks.

For easier paper removal, after stitching a seam, score the paper at the seam while trimming. When you're ready to remove the paper, dampen it slightly with a sponge or spray it once with a fine spray. Don't get it too wet. If you do, just press it a bit with a warm iron.
—Annie Toth, Moorpark, CA

You may wish to measure the finished block to be sure it is an accurate square and not distorted, though this is not usually necessary. On the rare occasion the block is distorted, "block" it by dampening it and then pinning it to a marked square of the correct size. Allow to dry. Press.

For easy paper removal, photocopy on a cheap-grade typing paper or onion skin paper, then press the finished block to scorch the paper. The paper becomes brittle and you can practically "snap" it off!
—Annie Toth, Moorpark, CA

BASTING AND QUILTING

Now your quilt top is ready to be made into a quilt.

1. Cut the backing and batting about 1" (2.5cm) larger all around than the quilt top.

2. Lay the backing wrong side up on a large, flat surface.

3. Lay the batting on top.

4. Lay the quilt, right side up, on top of the backing and batting.

5. Working from the center out, thread or safety-pin baste the three layers of the quilt "sandwich" together.

6. Quilt as desired.

7. Remove all basting stitches or remaining safety pins.

BINDING

You may bind your quilt—finish the outer edge with fabric—by either folding the backing to the front and stitching in place, or adding a separate strip of fabric.

NOTE: While they are a perfectly acceptable finish for a wall quilt, self-bindings may not be the best choice for a bed quilt. For these, use an attached binding strip. The double fabric of this type of binding will better withstand the wear and tear of everyday use.

SELF-BINDING

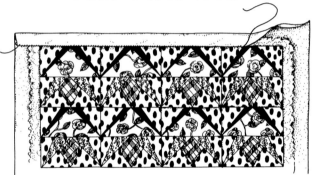

1. Trim the batting even with the quilt top. Trim the backing to ¾" (2cm) larger than the outer edge of the quilt all around.

2. Along one edge, fold the backing ¼" (6mm) to the front. Fold the backing to the front, over the edges of the batting and quilt top. Fold the sides in first, and slipstitch by hand or topstitch by machine. Repeat at top and bottom.

ATTACHED BINDING

1. Trim the batting and backing to be even with the quilt top.

2. To determine how long a binding to make, add the measurements of the four sides of your quilt top and an extra 8" (20cm).

3. Cut strips of binding along the straight, crosswise grain (there is some give to the crosswise grain) of your fabric. Use a diagonal seam to piece the strips together if necessary.

For a quilt show–quality finish, join the ends of the binding one-third away from the bottom right-hand edge of the quilt. This is the least noticeable join location and is the choice of award-winning quilters.

4. Wrong sides together, fold the seamed strips in half lengthwise. Press.

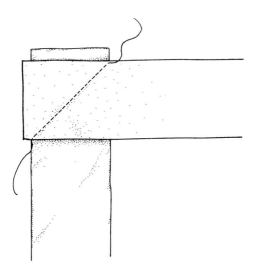

5. From right side and matching raw edges, place the binding strip along one edge of the quilt top. Machine stitch the binding to the quilt "sandwich," using a ¼" (6mm) seam allowance, depending on the desired finished binding width. Leave the first 3" (7.5cm) or so of the binding loose so that you can join the two ends of the binding later.

NOTE: The width of your binding strips is determined by the size of your quilt. For a wall hanging–size quilt, the finished binding that shows on the front surface should be about ¼" (6mm). The larger size of a bed quilt requires a finished binding of ½" (1.3cm) or wider for proper proportion. As an easy rule of thumb, cut your binding strips 1¾" (4.5cm) wide for wall hangings and 3¼" (8cm) wide for bed quilts.

6. At the first corner, stop stitching ¼" (6mm) from the edge of the quilt top. Raise the presser foot, but leave the needle down, in the fabric.

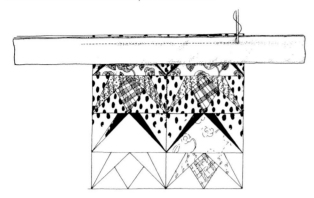

Pivot, and stitch diagonally to the corner of the quilt and off.

Hold the binding so the loose edge is straight up from the next side.

Fold the loose binding edge down, matching the raw edge to that of the next side of the quilt, and sew to the next corner.

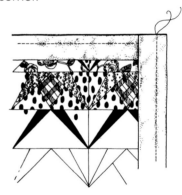

Repeat for the remaining corners.

7. When you approach about 4" (10cm) of the beginning of the binding, stop stitching. Match the ends of the binding as shown, opening them up to stitch them together along the diagonal. Refold and finish sewing the seam.

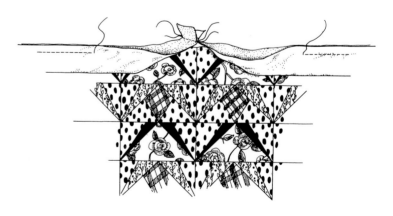

"Love is, above all, the gift of oneself."
—Jean Anouith
Ardele

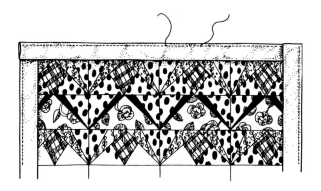

Press each short edge ¼" (6mm) to the wrong side twice. Topstitch.

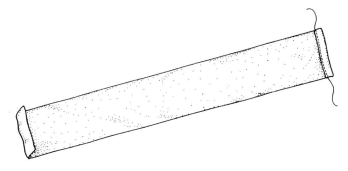

8. Fold the binding to the back of the quilt over the raw edges of the quilt "sandwich," covering the machine stitching at the back of the quilt. Slipstitch the binding in place.

2. Wrong sides together, fold the sleeve strip lengthwise in half. Center the raw edge of the strip along the top edge of the back of the quilt before attaching the binding. Baste.

3. Stitch the binding to the quilt as instructed above, securing the sleeve in the seam.

4. Slipstitch the bottom, folded edge of the sleeve to the back of the quilt.

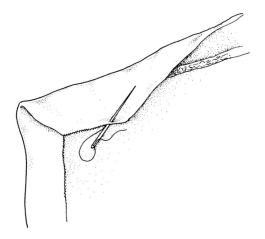

ADDING A SLEEVE FOR HANGING

To hang a small quilt on a wall, sew a simple sleeve to the back. A rod or ⅜"–¾" (1–2cm) dowel slipped into the sleeve provides the support to hang your quilt nicely. Cut the dowel 1" (2.5cm) longer than the sleeve.

1. Cut a strip of fabric 3½" (8.5cm) wide and as long as the width of your quilt less 1" (2.5cm) to 2" (5cm).

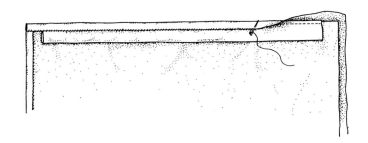

"I've memorized your face and the way you look at me... it melts my heart every time I think about it."
—Renée Duvall

YOU ARE INVITED...

The greatest pleasure in creating books is meeting people who share the quilting passion. The quilting family is a melting pot of those who love the art and craft of quilting, resulting in a sisterhood that brings me, for one, immense pleasure.

In this spirit, let's have a quilting bee of sorts through the mail. Whether you use the designs in this book or any other in the series, make these ideas a springboard for your creativity, or embark on your own, I'd love to see what you're making. Send me photos of your quilts and a letter about yourself and your quilting to the address below. Or contact me via the online service below. I look forward to meeting you.

JODIE DAVIS
Jodie Davis Publishing, Inc.
15 West 26th Street
New York, NY 10010
or via e-mail: CompuServe: 73522,2430

Linda is an active teacher and lecturer, and is always interested in hearing from readers and fellow quilters. If you would like more information on her classes or need help with any of the patterns in this book, please contact her.

Linda Hampton Schiffer
(at above address)
or via e-mail : quilter@lhsdesigns.jagunet.com

SOURCES

CLOTILDE
B3000
Louisiana, MO 63353-3000
(800) 772-2891
Catalog: Free
Sewing and quilting supplies.

CONNECTING THREADS
5750 N.E. Hassalo
Portland, OR 97213
(800) 574-6454
Catalog: Free
Quilting and related books, and more.

G STREET FABRICS
11854 Rockville Pike
Rockville, MD 20852
(301) 231-8998
If you ever get a chance, do visit this incredible Washington, D.C., landmark. The selection of fabric, notions, and trims is mind-boggling. The education department offers an intriguing selection of classes. Call for special requests and to inquire about their swatch service.

KEEPSAKE QUILTING
Route 25
P.O. Box 1618
Centre Harbor, NH 03226-1618
(800) 865-9458
(603) 253-8731
Catalog: Call for a free catalog
Pigma pens, books, fabric, huge selection of quilting supplies.

THE QUILT FARM
P.O. Box 7877
Saint Paul, MN 55107
(800) 435-6201
Catalog: Free
Books, fabrics, patterns, and quilting supplies.

QUILTS & OTHER COMFORTS
1 Quilters Lane
P.O. Box 4100
Golden, CO 80401-0100
(800) 881-6624
Catalog: Free
Books, large selection of quilting supplies.

BIBLIOGRAPHY

Fanning, Robbie, and Tony Fanning. *The Complete Book of Machine Quilting*. 2nd edition. Radnor, Penn.: Chilton Book Company, 1994.

Fones, Marianne, and Liz Porter. *Quilter's Complete Guide*. Birmingham, Ala.: Oxmoor House, 1993.

Hargrave, Harriet. *Heirloom Machine Quilting*. Lafayette, Calif.: C&T Publishing, 1990.

McKlvey, Susan. *Friendship's Offering: Techniques and Inspiration for Writing on Quilts*. Lafayette, Calif.: C&T Publishing, 1990.

Singer Sewing Reference Library. *Quilting by Machine*. Minnetonka, Minn.: Cy DeCosse Inc., 1990.

Thomas, Donna Lynn. *A Perfect Match: A Guide to Precise Machine Piecing*. Bothell, Wash.: That Patchwork Place, 1993.

INDEX

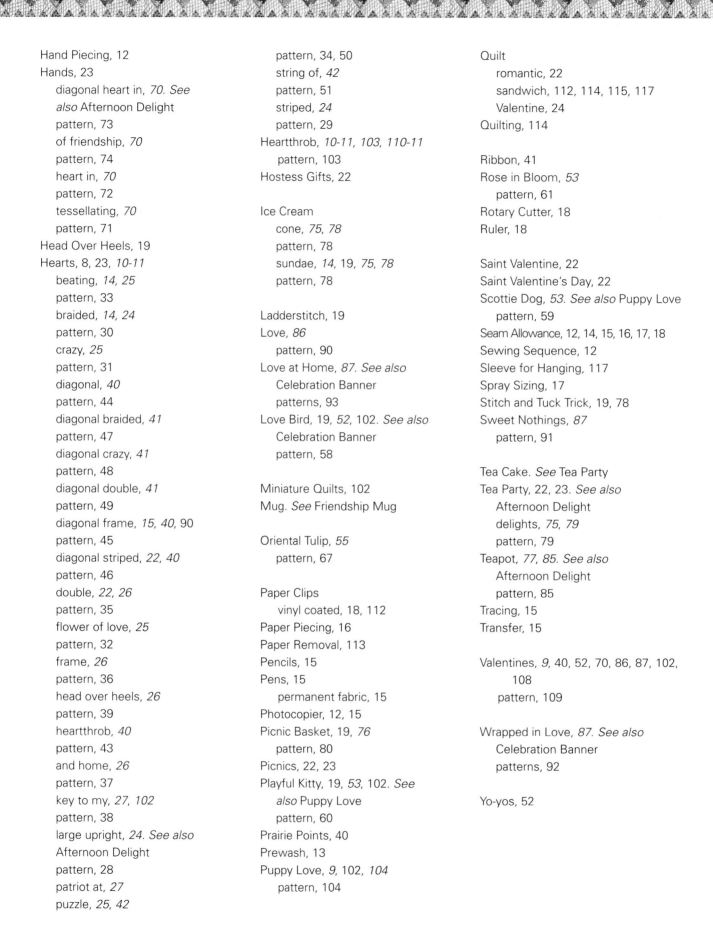